Spiritual Fruit Salad

Relationship with God

By

MAGDALENA EDMONSON

SPIRITUAL FRUIT SALAD
RELATIONSHIP WITH GOD

ISBN (Paperback): 979-8-89672-120-8
ISBN (Hardback): 979-8-89672-122-2
ISBN (Ebook): 979-8-89672-121-5

PROMINENT
BOOKS
EDGE

5830 E 2nd St, Ste 7000 #9983
Casper, WY 82609
USA

Contents

Introduction...v

Prologue: Fruit Salad ix

Chapter 1:   Getting to know You 1

Chapter 2:   The Waves of Love 22

Chapter 3:   The Joy of the Lord is my strength 66

Chapter 4:   My Peace I Give Unto You 90

Chapter 5:   Patience, His and Ours..115

Chapter 6:   Kindness 129

Chapter 7:   Goodness and Generosity......................................141

Chapter 8:   Gentleness..162

Chapter 9:   Faithfulness 180

Chapter 10: Self-control, Modesty, and Chastity.......................209

Epilogue: Who am I and why I am writing spiritual books?........233

Introduction

This is all my sister's fault. Have you heard that before? Actually, in this case it is a good thing. My first book had been in her possession for over two years before she started reading it, and she was impressed. She encouraged me to start writing again. But by now, I was legally blind, and could not read at all without special devices or programs for the visually impaired. If I tried to write, by hand, as I did for many years, neither I nor anyone else would be able to read it. But she said I could type, and it would be worthwhile. So, after many years, I started typing my conversations with God once more.

I had been faithfully getting up to pray every night for almost two years, as nighttime was my best time for prayer. Often it was very hard to concentrate even though I had few distractions. I needed to re-energize my prayer times, and thought I would take my sister's suggestion and try typing my prayers. The Lord met me on these pages, and began to reveal how we tend to misjudge and misunderstand Him. We know so little about God, and we imagine all the wrong things about each Person of the Trinity. No wonder so few people care to get close to the Triune God, much less love Him. He desires a close relationship with us. That is why He created us. But unless we get a better picture or idea of Him, we tend to back away or completely ignore.

My hope is that you will see how He is not at all like we tend to think of Him, but much, much better. I was taught that the "transcendence" of God is how much greater He is than we can imagine. Yes, He is all-knowing, all-powerful, all-present, creator of the universe, infinite in every way, beyond our understanding. But He is also "imminent," which means He is concerned with the smallest of details and cares about our lives. I will leave the "transcendence" to theologians who are much smarter than me. I need to tell you more about how His love, joy, peace, patience, kindness, gentleness, goodness, faithfulness, and self-control have touched my life. These are the fruits of the Spirit, which He exemplifies, and desires to grow within us as well. We are made in His image and likeness. We are to grow up to be more and more like Him. That is one of the reasons why Jesus came to the earth to show us what it all means. And why He sent His Holy Spirit to continue to guide us into such maturity.

Maturity has both good and bad aspects. The good is that it is possible, often an adventure, and can be very helpful. The bad part is that we keep at it and there is always more we need to learn. We don't quite reach the fullness of maturity as long as we live. But the other good news is that we get lots of help. As long as we don't give up, we can keep growing spiritually even if our bodies start deteriorating

As in my first book, <u>Grace and Gratitude, *Developing Personal Prayer*</u>, once I start sharing excerpts from my prayer journals, I will show my speaking to God in regular print, what I believe to be His response in **bold** print and any explanations in *italics*. Normally, I do not hear Him with my ears, but He manages to speak to me in my thoughts and often in my feelings as well. The more time I have spent in prayer, the more I recognize when He is speaking to me. But I still check with people smarter than me, to make sure I am not deceived by my own pride or delusions of grandeur.

While my first book was to encourage my readers to persevere in prayer, this one is meant to help deepen the loving two-way relationship with God. We often get stuck in one-way trends. We either think He will do whatever He wants regardless of what we ask, or we go on soliloquys and don't bother to listen for His replies. I have been guilty of both these. But it has gotten better. I hope it won't take you as long as it has taken me.

The fact is that God delights in revealing Himself to us. He knows us completely, as He has been with us throughout our lives, and knows every reason we are who we have become. But to have a relationship, we also need to know Him better. There are several places in Scripture where God's character is shown. The one I will focus on in this book is in Galatians 5:22-23. Since we seldom (or never) see God (and I often complain about His "invisibility thing) it is His character that we get to know and love. And, since we are made in His image and likeness, these are the things He wants us to develop or grow as well.

I thank all my teachers and guides who have nurtured me for so many years. I especially thank Mrs. Marion Rathbun who has graciously and patiently read and proofread my work.

Prologue

Fruit Salad

In Galatians 5:22-23 it says, "But the fruit of the Spirit is love, joy, peace, patience, kindness, goodness, faithfulness, gentleness, self-control; against such there is no law."

In the Catechism of the Catholic Church, Paragraph 1832 The fruits of the Spirit are perfections that the Holy Spirit forms in us as the first fruits of eternal glory. The tradition of the Church lists twelve of them: "charity, joy, peace, patience, kindness, goodness, generosity, gentleness, faithfulness, modesty, self-control, chastity."

Either way, they are called fruits. Fruits take a long time to grow. The seeds have to be rooted, planted, watered, fertilized. Once they sprout, the plants have to be protected, nurtured, and tended to. They grow in particular seasons. Now I don't think this is particular Church doctrine, but I suppose, before they are fully grown in us, the Holy Spirit provides us with a taste of each fruit so we can desire to have them grow within us. We experience many of these fruits as we grow up, before we have had any part in growing them. When all is done as it should be, we receive the love and gentleness of those around us. When, as children we get upset, we receive peace as someone consoles us. We receive joy in many ways. Many things can delight a small child. And so, we observe the other fruits in others, and are encouraged to practice them. Some come easier than others. I have valued and enjoyed practicing generosity, but had much trouble with self-control.

It is God who plants and nurtures the seeds and seedlings. He also provides others to care for, protect, and tend the process of growth. I can name many people in my life who modeled and taught me and made me desire to have these fruits growing inside me.

I have grown to love and appreciate the fruits of the Spirit. I even designed and crocheted a shawl many years ago with the Galatians version. I have made it several times, and gave them away, and they were appreciated.

There are times in our lives that we have to focus on one particular fruit. As a parent and as a teacher, patience is often scarce and really needs attention. As does self-control. Surprisingly, the Lord had to work long and hard to instill joy within me. In our current world, modesty and chastity have almost been lost, as they are clearly misunderstood. I consider them seedlings of self-control, just as I think generosity is very related to goodness. But we will explore all of the fruits in the following chapters.

The reason I named this book "Spiritual Fruit Salad" is that we need all of these fruits to live a good Christian life. They also are intrinsically the character of Jesus Christ. Though we can enjoy each fruit individually, they are meant to all be present in our lives. Most often, one fruit does not appear alone. Love, peace, and joy often go together. Patience, kindness, gentleness, and goodness are often hard to separate. Sometimes all work together, and the result is wonderful. Thus, we get a great mix, or a fruit salad.

Chapter 1

Getting to know You

In order to really love someone, it helps to get to know them well. My friend Anne used to say that we think we know God because we know about Him. Sort of like we know George Washington. We may have learned a lot about George, but having never actually met or talked with him, we don't really know him. It is a similar situation with God. We need to meet, spend time with, and talk with Him. He is not only what we heard about, or imagine Him to be like, but once we get to truly know Him, we find out what truly being loved and loving Him becomes.

When I restarted journaling my prayer life in June of 2022, I remembered that I had a "preparatory prayer" I used to say before each meditation when I went through the Spiritual Exercises of St. Ignatius many years ago. It was not as meaningful to me then, as I was simply obeying my spiritual director who said I should not barrel into prayer, but have a proper beginning and end. I searched and found a copy of it, printed it out in very large and bold letters, and began each nightly prayer time with it.

After a few weeks, I had committed it to memory, and, wonder of wonders, it began to have more and more meaning in my life. I do not know the author of the prayer, but am grateful.

Preparatory Prayer:
I offer You, my God, my whole self:
    my body with all its senses
    my soul with all its powers
    my heart with all its affections.

I offer myself to You completely during this time of prayer. Grant the grace that all I am and all I do here will be directed wholly and purely to loving and praising Your goodness.

Enlighten my mind that I may know You more intimately, that I may understand and feel vividly the matter I am about to consider. Inflame my heart that I may love You more deeply; and strengthen my will that I may better live my life according to Your direction and purpose.

Draw near to me, O Lord, in your own manner; reveal Yourself to me in your own way; and help me to remain open, listening and content here in Your presence.

Amen

Lord, I just had a thought – combined with a memory. I believe You are doing something a past spiritual director, Fr. Sanders, did in Your Name years ago. He took a prayer of dedication and turned it around. What I said to You, became what You were saying to me. I believe You are doing that with the preparatory prayer I say before each of these night prayer times. I almost have it memorized now – though I still have it available in case I get stuck. Lord, I will write it out now, with Your responses to each line.

I offer You, my God, my whole self

I offer you, my child, My whole Self

My body with all its senses

My Body, wounded for you, with all its senses

My soul with all its powers

My Soul with its infinite powers

My heart with all its affections

My Heart – My Sacred Heart – with infinite love for you.

I offer myself to You completely during this time of prayer

I offer Myself to you completely at all times

Grant the grace that all I am and all I do here will be directed wholly and purely to loving and praising Your goodness

I choose to give you all that I AM and all I do at all times and am wholly and purely directed to loving and caring for you and encouraging you.

Enlighten my mind that I may know You more intimately
My mind knows you totally and intimately
That I may understand and feel vividly the matter I am about to consider
I do understand and feel vividly all you are about to consider
Inflame my heart that I may love You more deeply
My heart is inflamed and I love you infinitely
And strengthen my will that I may better live my life according to Your direction and purpose
My Will is infinitely strong and I gave My life for you and continue to participate in your life according to My Father's direction and purpose.
Draw near to me, O Lord, in Your own manner
I have drawn near to you and ask you to draw near to Me whenever you can
Reveal Yourself to me in Your own way
I have revealed Myself to you in many ways and desire that you come to Me in all circumstances. Though I know you completely, I delight in hearing you reveal your inner thoughts and desires.
That I may remain open, listening and content here in Your Presence.
I AM always open, listening and content when you present yourself to Me.

Lord, how often we rattle off our memorized prayers, and never consider that You respond and are attentively listening. We act as if You are not really there – we don't consider what You say and do all the time for us. Forgive us, Lord. Help us to be more considerate of You.
I do forgive – and it delights My heart to have you see that I do respond so much more than My people realize.
Lord, it is once again that invisibility of Yours. You can and do see us, but we can only imagine Your response to us, and most of the time it never occurs to us to even imagine that You actually listen and answer us. You have revealed Yourself to me in this time of prayer.

Thank You. Help me to remember and realize all this as I pray in various ways.

Do not be discouraged if you find yourself rattling off your prayers as you have for years. I do not change. I listen even when you are not fully engaged. I AM. But if you sometimes take the time to consider My responses, that union with Me will continue to grow. When you converse with another person, it does not need to be elaborate and time-consuming. If you understand each other, it is conveyed automatically by your tone and facial expressions. In prayer, some of that is also automatic, but it is good to remember that I AM as real a person as you are, and respond whether or not you can see Me.

Lord, I thank You again. Hold me close. Nudge me occasionally so I remember to be more considerate of You.

I can do that. But you also have to live your life in the world. Do not be discouraged if you get caught up in the everyday ordinary things in your life. Remember that I have given you such a life and it is good to live it fully. But when you come to Me in prayer, don't forget I AM here.

You are indeed. I feel Your Presence. Thank You.

In my preparatory prayer, I offer You my soul with all its powers.
What are the powers of your soul?
I was wondering about that. I think the definition of soul is Mind, will, and emotions. There may be other definitions, but I don't know them.

Stick with the definition you know. Take them one at a time. What are the powers of the mind?
Memory; the ability to reason; to solve problems; imagination; the ability to picture things even when they cannot be seen; dreaming; the ability to traverse past, present, and future; that is all I can think of.

That is good enough. How about the will?

The ability to choose; to decide; to change; to act or not to act; I'm not sure if commanding is a part of it.

How about emotions?

There are so many. Liking, disliking, comfort, discomfort, security, insecurity, confidence, timidity, contentment, loneliness; it seems each emotion has a positive and a negative.

And the mind and the will have to work together to keep the emotions under control so the negative does not become the driving force. Do you understand the powers of the soul better now? There are more powers than you thought.

And You really made me think, too.

That is one of My powers.

Lord, as I pray my preparatory prayer, the last line touches me – "help me to remain open, listening and content here in Your Presence." Your Presence – You are here – it is so good to have You here. Content – Lord, You are already meeting all my needs – I cannot even think of wanting anything from You. At least not for myself. You are not here to work; You are here so I can listen to You and enjoy Your Presence. Lord, be comfortable here, stay and rest a while. I am listening if You want to speak.

Maggie, it is good to be content. It is also good to be listening. I thank you for your welcome. You are treating me like one of your sons. Just as you like being a mother, I like being a Son. Very few treat Me like a son. I am delighted that you now can think of Me in that way. It also brings a smile to My Father's face to see His Son loved as a Son. You were told in Scripture to figure out what pleases God. You have found one that does. We can rejoice together. Yes, I am Lord of lords and King of kings but I often referred to Myself as "Son of man." Few understood how much I value being a Son.

Lord, when my sons come here, it is different than when other guests come. I want my guests to be at home here, but my sons BELONG. Even though they have not lived here for many years, it is still their home, and they can fall asleep or do whatever they want here. You also belong here – this is Your house and home. It is so good to have You here. Let's rest now.

For several years, I had not written down my conversations with the Lord, as my eyesight had deteriorated that I could not read what I wrote. I did not stop praying, but often my mind would wander, and I felt like my connection with the Lord was not as it should be. Once my sister convinced me to start writing again, (actually now type) this was my first conversation with the Lord.

Dear Jesus, I want and need to please You. To connect with You – to thank You – to get so much closer to You. I want to hear and feel Your heartbeat. I want to be enveloped in Your arms. I want to know what I can still do for You. How I can still serve You despite my diminishments. There are many ways I try to come to You, but I still find that I am not treating You as I should or as You deserve. You do not complain, but I do. I need to listen better as I think You have been trying to tell me that things are not as bad as I think.

Maggie, you are in Martha mode, but can no longer work as the Martha used to. You would like to switch to the Mary mode but the Martha in you is agitated. You need lessons on how to become a Mary. Would you be willing to also be taught as you teach? *(Luke 10:39-42)*

Yes, Lord, I don't teach much any longer, but when I get a chance, I am happy to do it.

I will teach you. Seek Me. Look for My teaching. Sit at My feet and listen. I know you think you don't know how to do that. But writing again will help. I will ask you questions. Like I did in the Temple at age 12 but it will not be the 12-year-old that will be asking, but the Lord of lords and King of kings.

It is OK to write again? I thought You wanted to change my way of prayer since writing has become so difficult.

Are you having a difficult time writing now?

I guess not. And I do want to listen. I am conversing with You now. Much better than just sitting here letting my mind wander.

So, it is helpful!

Yes.

Are you convinced that I am here conversing with you?

Absolutely!

And are you now sure that I love you whether or not you can concentrate on Me?

It is not Your love for me that was bothering me, but my inability to respond to Your love.

You do not see things as I see them. Did you not learn that your desire to love Me is the same in My eyes as loving Me?

I did learn that long ago but have forgotten it. Or at least not sure I believed it.

Go ahead and choose to believe.

I think I can.

I do too. I will be with you through the night and the day. Feel My peace come upon you. My love for you is so much greater than you realize.

Thank You, Lord.

Dear Jesus, I don't think I am doing very well.

You want everything to be perfect instantly. Right now, you need to rejoice that your prayer times are redeemed. You have come to Me daily for almost two years now. I want you joyful and content. If all you can see in yourself are your faults and failings, then soon you will only see those things in others.

Lord, I don't want to do that.

I know. You need more balance. You can be very encouraging with others but miss the progress in your own life. You are still looking at Me as if I were hard to please. I am not. I see great good and can and will bring it about. Both in you and in those you care about. Remember that I have no problem with sin and failings. I forgive them. I want you to love yourself without being perfect or

puffed up. I allow the failures and work gently to improve you. Now is there anything else bothering you?

No, Lord, I think You covered it all.

That is what I do. Cover it all. Your assignment for today is JOY. Rejoice and be glad that I am with you. Do what you can – not what you can't. You are doing that with prayer. And I am delighted. Let it penetrate other parts of your life as well. See all the ways I love you. Your receptors of love need to open up. I do much more than hold you through the night. I am glad that you ask for and feel that I do, but there is more.

Is this another attitude transplant?

It is. You did not notice that you were becoming sad and negative. You need not be. I give you joy and peace and love, and all the other fruits of the Spirit. Use them, cultivate them. They are to grow in your life. They are meant for you to eat of them. That is why they are called fruits. Today you have two fruits in your refrigerator. Eat some. They will sweeten your disposition. And yes, you can still have some chocolate. The time will come when you will need to deny yourself of some things. But for now, I want to see joy in your life.

Lord, You are wonderful. Every time I expect a scolding, You shower me with kindness and great gifts. How can I ever thank You enough?

By accepting them with joy.

I'm not sure how well I did with being joyful yesterday. I did remember it a few times and kept busy doing what I could and not what I couldn't. My attitude was definitely a bit more positive. But here I am, grading myself again. What really matters is what You think.

I think it was good.

Lord Jesus, I had much trouble sleeping, but here I am complaining again.

I can handle complaining.

Lord, what I really need to say is "thank You" – that I can still function fairly well despite any problems with sleep, and that my schedule allows for naps if I need them.

Lord, I feel the joy of being able to discuss something so trivial with You.

It is good. Not everything is earth-shaking. But I am here and delight in conversing with you. Enjoy the peace and bring Me all your cares, no matter how great or small.

Thank you, Lord.

After a prayer time when I spent a long time praying for family and friends:

Keep interceding for others as you have been. It is helpful. You do not see that your prayers are valuable or effective, but I see a bigger picture than you can. You do not need to see the results, but you do need to believe that they exist. Here is where the gift of faith comes in.

With your eyesight, you understand better than most people that even when you don't see something, it is there. You don't see all the details of things you do but can tell if the desired result is better than when you started.

The things you work on, are mostly things you do by yourself. What you are crocheting, will turn out well if you keep at it. You correct any mistakes along the way, and it is good. But with your prayers, it is as if you joined with many other people to work on a project and each one does only a small part of it. Like a quilting bee you have seen in Amish country. Each person focuses on their own portion of the project, and eventually a beautiful thing emerges.

I have given you only a portion of the prayers needed to bring healing to both the nation and to those you pray for. If you

do your part, it will come together and will be good. If you make a mistake, or skip an important step, others will help and it will still work out. But if you do your part well, and help those around you as needed, the finished product will be completed more easily. You do not have to do it all. Many hands work toward the same goal. It is unity. I value unity.

Keep on praying. Not only does it work toward what is good and desirable, but it continues to bring you closer to Me. And I draw closer to you, listening intently to your every word and thought. You don't expect Me to lean closer to listen to you. You imagine Me to be busy with more important matters, but I can do both. There are advantages to Deity.

Yes, we both are smiling now. But the lesson is that I come close and hear and feel and respond to your prayers. Sometimes you don't even have the words, but I know what you mean. It is good.

Enjoy My love and care and attentiveness to you.

Thank You, Lord. I get the picture of You leaning down to have a little child whisper in Your ear. And there is a smile on Your face just happy to have the child wanting to tell you something. I am that child.

Dear Jesus, I remember many years ago leaving our prayer meeting very frustrated. I practically yelled at You about how awful it was that the blind came into our prayer meeting and left still blind. The lame left still lame, and Your healing power was nowhere to be seen. I don't remember Your response, but eventually I figured that the problem was not at Your end, but ours. We were not good enough, or holy enough, or there must be something lacking in us.

Through the intervening years, You calmed me down enough that I am not angry about it all anymore, but still wonder what we still lack. One of the answers I hear, is that the proper time is now approaching where Your healing Hand will again be manifested in signs and wonders. I hope whatever we were lacking has passed, and we can indeed walk in Your power.

I still do not understand the acceptance of suffering vs. seeking Your healing. You healed others but suffered and died. But then You rose from the dead. You raised Lazarus, but St. Joseph died before You started Your ministry. Sometimes it says in Scripture that You healed them all, and at other times, only some were healed. I am sure You have Your reasons, and do not need my understanding or approval, but You see how it is confusing.

I do indeed see how confusing it is. Faith, trust, hope, perseverance, are very important. They do not rely on complete understanding. Many of My disciples left me when they did not understand the Bread of Life discourse. But some did not leave, they grew in faith and persevered even unto death. Did they understand completely? No, but they had a strong enough relationship with Me that they were willing to wait for the understanding until I would give it to them. *(John 6:55-71)*

It is good to seek understanding, but it is not the most important aspect of your life. Will you understand everything in this life? No, but you do understand much more than you did in the past. You have seen how I bring good out of the most difficult of situations. You have seen both natural and supernatural things and understand that I work through both. You have learned that though your prayers are valuable and helpful, they do not twist My arms to do exactly what you desire.

You have seen that I often have a bigger picture and have grown to trust My judgments. You have asked me questions and I have sometimes answered them directly, and at other times made you wait for the answers. But your love for Me has grown, and your doubts have disappeared. It is not wrong to ask questions, but not all questions will be answered to your complete satisfaction in this life.

This is why I value the childlike faith. A small child does not understand everything but is still filled with awe and wonder. Children discover and learn constantly. I have given you a teach-

able heart, and you are still learning and asking questions. It is good. Watch and see what I do.

Continue doing what you know are good things. Keep praying and seeking My Will. I will not disappoint you. I reveal Myself to you a little at a time. Otherwise, you would be overwhelmed. I don't tell you everything at once. But I am with you and I help you even when you don't understand. Keep trusting Me.

Thank You, Lord. I do trust You, and I don't have to understand everything. I am grateful that You guide me step by step. I do love You and know Your ways are much better than I could possibly handle. I am glad I asked You to help me trust You completely. You are doing that.

I really like fresh figs. Many years ago, my grand-nephew bought me a tiny fig tree, and I named it Figgy. For seven years, (the proper time for fig trees) it bore no fruit. When it finally did, we only found three figs that year. This was the eighth year, and it still only produced a few.

Lord, thank You also for five more figs from Figgy. They are very good. We waited a long time but finally get some fruit. Lord, how very long time You have had to wait for some of us to produce good fruit.

Yes, that is true, but I have an advantage. I can see the end from the beginning. All those years you waited you were not sure there would ever be fruit. But even if there is but a few figs, it is a reason to rejoice. I rejoice at even a small harvest. But the time will come when the harvest will be great as well. I also rejoice when I find good fruit. Sometimes you have to search for it. It is hiding under a lot of leaves. There is much you can learn from a fig tree. Many people wonder why I cursed that one that did not have fruit out of season. What do you think? I never understood it, either. Did You see something others could not? Was there a disease or parasite that only You knew about? Or was there a different lesson in that which had nothing to do with the tree itself? *(Mark 11:12-14: 20-25)*

Now you are understanding better. My disciples needed to learn that every word has an effect. You also need to learn that. What seems to be a thoughtless comment, can have a surprising result, positive or negative. I did not hate fig trees. I knew it was not the season for figs. But they saw that even what seemed to be an off-hand statement had serious consequences. You have seen this in your own life. You have had to repent and apologize for comments that were meant to be funny but produced pain instead. You have seen it especially in the lives of young people. It is a good reason to weigh your words before they come out.

Lord, I thank You for this lesson. I certainly was not expecting it. You use such mundane things to teach such important lessons. Thank You for my fig tree. Thank You for that withered one in Your own time. It may not have ever produced figs, but it has produced a great lesson for us to watch what we say. Thus, in a way, it has produced very good fruit.

This is what I do. Even what seems to be disastrous, I can bring good out of it.

Dear Jesus, I thank You for the teaching yesterday about the fig tree. I need to look it up to see what else You said at that time. In Matt 21:18-22 is another mention of the same story. It is just as I thought. The next part is You telling the disciples that if they have faith, they can tell a mountain to be cast into the sea and it will happen. Lord, I believe You are answering my question about why our people do not get healed at our services. Our faith has grown so weak, that we doubt. So how can our faith grow enough to be effective?

You know that faith is a gift. But it is not a thing that just sits on a shelf totally static. It is living and can grow. It must be fed and watered. In other words, it grows with use. Your faith has grown much over the years. Remember when it was not much more than a desire? But now it is securely planted and growing. But there are weeds nearby that need to be removed. Not only in your own life, but in the life of the Church.

The spiritual messages you listen to, they are feeding your faith. When you see someone healed, it is like a fine shower making your faith grow. As your prayers for others are effective, you are more likely to pray for more issues. Taking authority over evil, also gives growth. The mountain that is to be taken up and cast into the sea, is the evil that is in the way of My Will in your life and in the world.

Cursing is not always a bad thing to do. But it must be the evil that needs to be cursed. And when cursed with faith, it will be removed. Moses placed before the people, life and death, blessing and cursing. He advised them to choose life. You also have choices. Bless people. Curse evil. Many get it backwards.

That is why you need to stay in constant contact with Me. I will guide you and show you how to maneuver when things get confusing. I also had to stay in constant contact with My Father while on earth. That is why I needed to get away and pray at times. You are now doing that. Your faith is growing. Doubt is shriveling up. The good news is that I am not finished with you yet.

As you continue to seek Me and My Will, you will find it more easily. As you ask your questions and My help, you will receive it more readily. As you knock the doors will open. I promised it all. It is yours.

Remember that the farmer plants the seed, but it is God that provides the growth. It is not your actions that grow your faith, but Mine. I do want your faith to be strong and powerful, but it has to be surrounded with other virtues to protect it. Like humility, perseverance, courage, hope, and love. I have planted these within you, and only I know the right conditions for optimal growth. Let Me be in charge.

I see that we are back to submission, surrender, and supplication; but with trust and joy, not fear and dread.

Good. You got the message.

I was able to listen to a message on James 4:6-10. That we need to submit to You and then, the devil will flee when we resist him. This sort-of answers my complaint of why we seem to lack the power to do the greater things that You spoke about. Both our faith and our submission need to increase. Lord, please help my faith and submission to grow exponentially. The three s's seem to be very important: submission, surrender, and supplication.

Yes, they are. But as they are being perfected in you, I can still work great things through you even if they are not yet fully developed. Just because you do not see great miracles, it does not mean that I am not using you. As you have seen in your own life, I can use the most imperfect prayers you haltingly utter to bring about great change.

Remember when you were told to thank Me for your parents? That little insincere prayer changed the rest of your life with your parents. My power is great even in your weakness. But it does not mean that I want you to remain weak. I am continually strengthening you as you seek and find Me in all situations.

The desire you have to do greater things is from Me. As you learn more submission and surrender, your humility will also increase, and you will have more grace as it is given to the humble. Your spiritual hearing will also increase and you will be able to discern My Will in each situation. When your prayers are united to My Will, great things happen.

This is why you have been seeking union with Me. I put that desire in your heart. I am also fulfilling it a little at a time. But even if it is slower than you would like, it is happening. Do not doubt or be discouraged. Both My love and power are much greater than you can imagine.

Thank You, Lord.

Nighttime prayer is a good time to draw near to Me so I will draw near to you. I value these times during the night, and I long to be as close to you all day as well. I know you desire it, too. Be

assured that total union with Me is possible and happening. It just proceeds slowly so you are not overwhelmed.

Slow growth is good. There are so many small victories during slow growth that would be missed if things happened all at once. This is why recovery after an illness or some catastrophe happens in small increments. Every bit of progress is an occasion to rejoice. The process gives a chance for relationships to develop. Not just relationship with Me, but with others as well.

Miracles are rare for a reason. They are quick and though spectacular; they do not allow for the process of small victories. The natural progression of healing and building has its purpose. It is what I use in most cases. That is why the supernatural has the prefix of super.

Lord, I do thank You for Your natural healing and growing in my life. Help me to be more patient with the way You do things.

You are getting there. You thought you were patient, yet yesterday you had a hard time in the math lesson. You knew I was there enjoying the scene. You did OK. And the whole lesson was completed in time. But it was difficult. Through the struggle, your patience was growing, and your love for your student and understanding of his way of doing things also increased.

Thank You, Lord. I guess there is more progress than I was aware of.

That is true, and often the case.

How do you like My using you the past few days?

I'm not sure I noticed. But now that I think of it, there have been times I see You giving me the opportunity to be of service. Thank You. It seems that when You present me with such opportunities, I lose track of time and feel I need to finish the job well. It does not even occur to me that You provided the job. Tutoring is like that. So are some phone calls with Your troubled folks, and visits with sick people. All this is Your involvement in my life? Am I really doing Your will in these cases?

You seem surprised. I have been using you in this way for many years. Just because it seems so natural to be doing these things, does not mean that it is not My Will. Not all of My Will is difficult, not everything merits "the agony in the garden." Was I not doing My Father's will when preaching or healing? There can be joy and satisfaction, not just trepidation. And even when there was trepidation, it says in Scripture that it was for the joy set before Me that I endured the Cross.

When I ask you to do something that you find scary, I will always provide you with a promise of good coming out of it. There needs to be some trust on your part for that. It is in these times of natural service that I am teaching you that trust. You are learning it well. Fear not. I continue to guide you, use you, teach you, and most of all, love you.

Wow! All I can say is thank You.

After telling the Lord all my plans for the following week, I continued:

Of course, this is all contingent on Your plans, as You can change or cancel any plans I make. Lord, now I do have a burning question. There seems to be a tightrope of making plans and yet being submitted to Your Will.

I can answer that one. It has a lot to do with how attached you are to your plans. Just as you can get attached to wealth or other things, you have a tendency to get attached to your plans. You get upset when things don't work out the way you thought they would. Submission does not mean you leave all planning to Me or someone else, it means that you can sweetly handle any changes when necessary. Some changes can be disappointing, but others can be delightful. Submission can mean being ready for surprises.

Not all surprises are difficult or distasteful. There is a tendency to think of submission only in a negative way. When you consult Me about what to do during the day, I do not wear you out. I give you all the rest you need, and do not require anything too hard for you. Yet you think submission to Me would be fore like the taskmasters of Egypt. I do not take away your joy, I provide it. I want you joyful. Submission is not restrictive, but freeing. I know how to make you happy. I want to do so.

Yes, I also teach you and let you experience difficulties, but the goal is always for your benefit. I do not do anything out of meanness. Yet so many people think everything involving My Will is going to be terrible. What do people think of when they say things are an "Act of God?" They think of major natural disasters. Earthquakes, floods, lightning and fire. Yes, I allow those things, but My unnoticed acts are the ones that people attribute to good luck or happenstance. My goodness goes unnoticed while disasters are credited to Me.

Parents and those in authority often have the same issues. Obedience has a bad reputation just as submission. Surrender is even worse. But when the one in charge is all-good, submission, surrender, and obedience are pathways to freedom and joy. And remember that I am a master at bringing good out of even the worst disasters.

Lord, You do reveal Yourself when we are willing to listen. I am so sorry for all the ways I have accepted the world's view of You. We have a hard time remembering Your goodness. We expect wrath and vengeance when dealing with You. Fear of God should be awe and wonder, but we mostly use the word fear as being afraid. You keep telling us not to be afraid, yet we miss that. Thank You for Your awesome goodness.

How often in the Psalms it tells us to Praise the Lord. I am beginning to understand that praising You is not just saying words of praise but knowing with every particle of our being that You are so loving and caring and desire only what is good for us. Words of praise seemed empty to me before. Now that I know You better, I can fill them with the knowledge of the truth they are to contain. You are awesome. Your power is for good. Your strength is for our benefit. Your plans are perfect. You are worthy of all our love and praise.

You asked Me to reveal Myself. I am delighted that you understand. You did not understand in your teens how one can love a God. Now you see so much more. You need to know Me as I am, not as the world thinks of Me. Then loving Me is natural and easy. Submission and surrender and obedience become delightful. Union is happening. Rejoice!

One day, I was about to do one thing while I thought the Lord was telling me to do another, I stopped in my tracks, and did as He said.

I felt I was being obedient, and it was good.

And it was not difficult or burdensome. This is also union. Not the warm fuzzy kind, but real none-the-less. The joy is there along with the love and peace. Even self-control is happening. In fact, all of the fruits can be found in this union. You were right many years ago, when You demanded total union with Me, that you had no idea what that meant. But now that you are experiencing it, it does not look as mysterious or impossible as you expected.

And I am grateful.

Lord, I don't want to be so busy that all I can talk to You about is my schedule. I need to connect with You about more than the relatively insignificant parts of my life. Would You provide a topic?

I would. Yesterday you had two conversations that started awkwardly, but eventually turned out well. Prayer can be like that. At first, you are grasping for words, and stick to mundane issues. But eventually, more serious topics emerge, and a new and closer connection comes. Do not be put off by the awkwardness of the beginning.

The visit with a sick friend was difficult yesterday. You expected a pleasant birthday celebration combined with prayer and levity. She was not in such a shape as to either enjoy anything or be enjoyable. It was the most fractured prayer you have ever prayed, and there was not really any celebration. Yet, all 8 people involved were somehow blessed, and the prayers were still effective, despite all the interruptions. You saw that though she had been making progress in recovery, yesterday was definitely several steps backwards. They endure, but everyone around them also endures, and hopefully learns from the experience. Compassion is a good result. It grows in those who care for the person going through the difficulty. Many virtues were on display yesterday. Though none of the eight people present felt edified, I saw patience, compassion, love, kindness, forbearance, faithfulness, gentleness, goodness, self-control, just about all the fruits of the Spirit. I delight in seeing My people display good fruit.

Growth happens when you are not aware of it. Have you not grown through caring for others? You have seen how several of your students who had family members that were somehow disabled, were gentler and kinder than others. The beauty of their character developed through the difficulties they encountered through caring for others. Few people understand that disabilities are not just painful and unfortunate but are a means of character development for many others around the one who is disabled. This is how I bring good out of any difficult situation.

Remember when once you confessed your difficulties to a kind friend, and you were surprised that he said that the problems you were having were not for you. They were to teach others. You wondered about it then but now you see what he meant. Everything that happens has larger repercussions than immediately obvious.

Like a rock being thrown into water, there are circles of change all around and the ripples go much farther than expected. This is why you are encouraged not to grow weary of well-doing. It has ripples you may never notice, yet they do what I desire in many lives.

How was that for an awkward beginning?

Lord, You are awesome! I had no thoughts of how to pray tonight. Yet You revealed great truths. Thank You.

I was encouraged to consider the Fatherhood of God. You have long ago healed my concept of fatherhood and I thank You. I have been aware through the years of the good qualities of various fathers, and I think my image of God the Father is much better. But as I read Col. 1:15-20, it is more about You than the Father. I suppose that is why You said that if we have seen You, we have seen the Father. As You and the Father are one, so You and I both desire that I may be one with You. Union! The cry of my heart is also the cry of Your heart.

Are you encouraged by this? Not only the cry of My heart, but also the cry of My Father's heart. Union is what creation is all about. Just as you felt that the inspirations you received in past years through your writing were too good to keep to yourself and should be shared with others, so the Father felt union was too good not to be shared. In the Trinity, there is perfect union. That is the goal of creation. In heaven, there is perfect union. On earth, not so much. But that is the goal. And despite all the setbacks, there is progress. Look for this progress. There is wheat among the tares.

Thank You, Lord. There is, indeed.

Chapter 2

The Waves of Love

During my senior year in high school, I decided to go on a "quest." It was 1965, and a popular musical playing was "The Man of La Mancha." One of the songs was all about his "quest." Since the age of 11, I had wanted to give my life to God as a nun. But I had a question in the back of my mind as to whether I actually loved God. I was exceedingly grateful to him for the extraordinary way He brought us to this country when we escaped from Communism in Hungary. I felt I owed Him my life. But how does one love a God? I knew how to love people, and even animals, but how does one love a God whom we cannot see? My quest was to discover how one can love an invisible God.

There were few people I told about my quest. One was a teacher at the church I attended, but not only could he give me no answer, he quit that very week, and I never saw him again. If I mentioned it to anyone else, I just got a blank stare, and the subject was never mentioned again. I thought I should surely be able to figure it all out before graduation, but the answer did not come to me.

After graduation, life got busy and interesting and the quest receded to the far back corner of my mind. It was still there, but set aside. I got a job, unexpectedly fell in love, went to college for a year, got married, worked again for a while, finished college, and started teaching math. During this time, I strayed from my faith, and hardly even thought of God.

Then our first son was born. I did not even know why I wanted a child, as I had only heard of all the problems with having kids. I knew about sleepless nights, dirty diapers, crying babies, childhood illnesses, responsibilities, bad behavior, costs, and such things. But I still wanted a baby. One day, while I was pregnant, my husband and I were at a restaurant and a mother with two unruly children was there. I remember thinking, "Why in the world did I want children at all?" But I did, and the day finally came when our first son came into the world.

Absolute joy enveloped me. The warmth of that little bundle, the beauty of such a miraculous creation having come out of me, the pride and admiration of my husband who was there to see how difficult childbirth was; these were unexpected but welcome experiences. Then there were others, too. I found out that my son could be quite unhappy and crying, but as soon as I picked him up, he was suddenly happy and comfortable. Then the beauty of that first smile, and soon the music of his laughter. I began to rediscover the world through his development. Watching him discover his own hand movements, each new feat of strength, turning over, sitting up, drinking from a cup, speaking an understandable word, so many wonders. Yes, there were responsibilities and some not so great, but overall, motherhood was a lot better than I had imagined. Once again, love surprised me.

Neither my husband nor I were churchgoers by this time. I decided for the baby's sake to try going back to church again. It was difficult at first, as I could not honestly participate in what I thought I no longer believed. I knew I could not say the Creed, as that would have been a lie. Eventually, through a series of divine interventions, I re-discovered my faith, and my quest was renewed.

It took several months, but now the desire to know and love God had become strong within me. I received the "baptism of the Holy Spirit," and with it a thirst for Scripture. While studying the book of John, I came across John 14:15, "If you love Me, you will keep My commandments." There was my answer. Keeping His commandments. I could do that, I thought. By now, my relationship with my parents was better, and I could honor them. I did not kill, steal, lie, commit adultery, or even covet anything or anyone. I did not use God's name in vain, I went to church on Sundays. But did I love Him with all my heart, soul, mind, and strength? I still was not sure. But this was progress.

I kept studying and learning as much as I could while raising my family. By now I had three sons, and life was pretty busy. But when my husband was willing to let me go for a few days, I would go to a nearby retreat house to pursue my relationship with God. I read many books on prayer and listened to teachings wherever I could find them, and really wanted to love God as He deserved, but I was not convinced that I really did.

On one of these retreats, as the retreat house was on a hill overlooking the Potomac River, I started walking down to the river shore, and the thought came to my mind, "I love you." By now I knew God could speak to me in my thoughts, so I responded, "That's nice." Then the same thought came back, and my response was the same. By the third time, I realized that my response was rather weak at best, and thought I needed to do better than that. But when I got down to the river, the waves were rather large, and relentlessly hitting the shore. What I realized was the Lord speaking to me in my thoughts came again, explaining, "Each wave is My telling you that I love you. And just as the waves cannot stop coming to the shore, neither can I stop loving you."

He was not concerned with my feeble responses; He simply wanted me to be assured of His love for me. I stopped trying to improve my response, and simply marveled at His kindness, gentleness, and love.

It took another retreat and another descent down to the river, when I had the courage to ask Him a question about love. I explained to Him, as if He did not know, that I knew He loved me, but how can I love Him back? Then He showed me how when a wave comes to the shore, all the water recedes back into the river in little ripples. I suddenly understood. The Scripture Matt 25:40 came to me "'Truly, I say to you, as you did it to one of the least of these my brethren, you did it to me." He went on, every little kindness you do for others, is like one of these little ripples of water going back into the river. As My waves of love reach you on the shore, so do those ripples reach Me back in the deep. Your love for Me may not look as impressive as the waves coming to the shore, but they are all I want. I also said in John 15:12, "This is my commandment, that you love one another as I have loved you."

All of that made sense, and I continued to busy myself caring for family, friends, and strangers. Yet I still was not satisfied. I enjoyed loving others, but I wanted to love Him. I wanted to fall head-over-heels in love with the Triune God. That took many more years.

Very often during those years, I was totally convinced that He loved me. Once I chose to believe that He was Who He and the Bible said He was, He demonstrated His love for me in so many unmistakable ways that there was no doubt possible. But I still was not convinced that I loved Him. Or even that I was capable of loving My invisible God. But I kept talking to Him, and sought to know Him better. He kept telling me that even my desire to love Him was a big part of love, but I still felt totally inadequate.

He had to disable me to the point that I could no longer do the things I thought were loving to others, and thus to Him. I became lame, weak, almost blind, and pretty desolate. Yet I knew He loved me.

Finally, I started once again to seek to know Him. He began to reveal Himself to me in ways I had not considered before. Jesus showed me how since I was made in His image and likeness, many of the things I experienced, He had also felt in His own life on earth. I began to see His humanness, and realized how much He understood all my struggles. I started consulting Him before I tried to ask anyone else about how to handle certain situations. My relationship with Him became different.

He was more approachable than our society gives Him credit for. He always welcomed me and treated me with kindness, patience, gentleness, and all the fruits of the Spirit. I began to want to do the same for Him. I wanted to soothe His frazzled nerves, put my arms around Him, wipe away His tears. I learned to appreciate any opportunities He gave me to serve Him, whether by just spending time with Him alone, or helping someone He sent to me.

Have I arrived at loving Him as He deserves? Not likely. I still have so much to learn. I still mess up a lot. So many times I forget to consult Him, forget He is with me, and ignore His promptings. But it is better than it used to be. And I am grateful that He will continue to draw me closer to Him until He takes me home.

You started to think of the progression of your love for Me. It is good to recount that.

My first recollection of wanting to love You was when I was receiving instruction for First Communion. The priest that secretly came to teach me in Communist Hungary, must have done a really good job, as I asked my mother if there were such people that tell others about You. I had never heard of missionaries before but had a desire to be one.

During our escape from Hungary, I realized that we needed Your help, and promised You that if we survived, I would pray an Our Father every time I remembered how You led and protected us. I was not able to keep that promise and had often felt bad about it.

The story of my family's escape from Hungary was written by John Hersey as the second chapter in his book, Here to Stay.

At age 11, when I read Mr. Hersey's account of our escape, I was overwhelmed with gratitude at how powerfully You saved us and brought us here, and felt I needed to repay You by giving my life to You. The only way I thought I could do that was to become a nun, so for the next eight years, I kept that as my goal in life.

But during my senior year, I had a big question. I knew how to love people, even those who were not all that lovable, but how does one love a God, Whom we could not see? I thought for sure I would figure it out within that year of high school, but no-one I asked could give me an answer. I tucked that thought into the back of my mind, and graduated, went to work, fell in love, got married, gave up my faith, got a college degree, went to work again, and had our first son. You soon brought the desire within me to come back to You, and slowly, ever so slowly, You revealed Yourself to me. I still did not know how to love You, but that quest returned.

You baptized me with Your Holy Spirit and gave me such a thirst for knowing about You, that I kept studying and searching and the desire to love You continued to grow. I finally thought I figured out how to love You when I came upon the Scripture, "If you love Me, keep My commandments." I strove to keep Your commandments, and continued to learn of You. I rededicated my life to You often but had a hard time believing that I actually loved You. I did have fleeting moments of devotion, and You were gracious enough to keep speaking to me whenever I came to You, but I could not maintain a disciplined or regular prayer life.

Yet You did not abandon me, and gave me sporadic growth spurts, and my book emerged. I had wonderful retreats where I began to know You better, and even began to feel a bit of love for You, all the while fully understanding that Your love for me was very great. My relationship with You may not have been constant but You kept drawing me back again and again. And each time I finally returned to seek You, You rewarded my efforts with Your grace and love.

I responded the best I could, but still doubted that I loved You. I never doubted that You loved me, and I was always grateful for that, but I felt totally inadequate in my response.

When You allowed me to enter the convent and allowed me to feel I was finally truly giving my life to You, my prayer life dried up, such as it was. Though I was serving You with all my heart and strength, I could not communicate with You as well as I had before I became a nun. You rescued me once again, though I took it as rejection, not by You, but by the order.

Then You gave me the joy and opportunity to care for my mother, and I knew it was Your Will, and I was delighted to finally be at the center of Your Will. After she passed, I fell head-over-heels in love with a gentleman, and was delighted that I was still able to love anyone so completely. But that also ended up with rejection, and I had no-one else to turn to but You. You did provide me with wonderful counselors, but only You could heal my heart. And You did.

The pandemic came, and having little else to do, I received the inspiration to compile my book, and You even gave me help with editing it. Then when the politics in the country were difficult, I finally committed to a daily prayer time, and You very kindly kept me faithful to it.

Eventually, I was encouraged to start writing again, and You once again met me in my writing. You have revealed Yourself to me in such tender and wonderful ways, that I now have no doubts that I love You. I know You much better than ever before, and You have removed a lot of my misconceptions about You. Your goodness completely overwhelms me, and I am very grateful. I am also very thankful that You receive my love, even as imperfect as it still is, and continue to reveal Yourself to me and help my love for You grow.

Now you also see how good it is that I see the end from the beginning. I knew from the beginning that your love was going to mature. And you also knew it was worth seeking what you had heard was possible. You knew others had been able to not only believe they loved Me, but actually feel that love. Now that you know you can also feel it, the next step is to let it become constant. That it should become the motivating force of every moment of your life. That, too, is possible, though you do not experience it yet. I will keep loving and teaching you until that also becomes a reality.

Remember when I told you that you were afraid to love Me? Now you are afraid to receive My love. I finally convinced you that you do love Me. The next step is to recognize and receive and thoroughly enjoy the love I shower upon you. Right now, you are bombarded with the feelings of unworthiness and recrimination. That is not from Me. It is to be fought. Union with Me is full of joy and peace. Receive My gifts. They have no strings attached. I want you free and happy.

Lord, I feel Your Presence. Thank You. Let me go and bask in it.

My arms are ready for you to be enveloped in them. Receive the garment of praise for that spirit of heaviness you have been carrying. And throw the heaviness out. It does not become you.

Thank You, Lord. I go with a smile on my face.

That is much better.

Lord, I really want to thank You for the loving and kind way You meet me each night. I have begun to feel intimacy With You that I had heard about, desired, but thought would never happen to me.

I had to wait until you were no longer afraid of loving Me. My love for you has always been much more intense than you could receive. There is still more than you now understand. I have longed for the opportunity to have you experience the greater depths of My love.

Lord, I get a picture of a baby sea turtle on the shore of the ocean. It longs to enter the water but hesitates at the edge. Finally, it dares to enter and finds that it is where it was meant to be.

Yes, you are meant to be in the ocean of My love. Not just watching the waves on the shore.

Lord, I don't even know how to respond. Words are not coming, but somehow, I seem to understand. I can only thank You.

That is perfectly all right. Stay with that attitude. It is good.

It is a different thing to desire or want something and living in possession of it. It is somewhat like pregnancy. There is a long waiting period, and finally the baby emerges, and then life changes dramatically. The adjustment is at the same time quick and gradual. There is a vast difference between being an expectant mother and being a mother.

You find yourself in such a situation. You have had dreams where you seemed to have a child but forgot to do some important things that should have been done. In reality, however, the child would make enough noise, that you could not forget. Living in union with your God is similar but not the same. It will require all the fruits of the Spirit as well as the beatitudes. But the demands of such a life are inward, not outward.

I will not make noise to get your attention. But I will want your attention. You will also want My attention, and I will respond. Look to Me. See how I respond to you and imitate Me in responding to My calls. And don't forget to rejoice. You will have all the help you need.

Lord, I don't even know how to respond. There are several emotions running through me. I am not known for humility, yet I feel humbled by Your goodness. Yes, there is joy, too. And the sincere desire not to mess this up. Not quite a fear, but similar.

It is all good and natural. Trust Me to lead you through all the changes. Remember that I am in control.

And I am grateful that You are.

Dear Jesus, have I lost my "First love" for You? Am I considering my own comfort more important than coming to You? I used to be grateful that You woke me up around 3:00 AM to come to You. Now it seems to be a struggle every time I wake up whether I should go back to sleep or come to pray. I used to be determined not to be robbed of my time alone with You. Now, I cannot think of how to pray if my computer is not working.

Here I am, repenting again. You don't deserve to be treated this way. You have not changed. Your love and care continue to sustain me, regardless of my attitudes. I think I need one of Your attitude transplants.

Done. You have been trying to be in Martha mode, but there is not enough Martha-type work to be done. You cannot complain that you have too much to do, as there is no-one to serve. So now, replace the complaining with gratitude. Listen more for My voice than your body's discomforts. Do not allow yourself to be robbed of joy and peace. It is such a simple turn. Turn from focusing on yourself, to focusing on Me. I do provide all that you need, but not all that you want.

Lord most of the time I don't even know what I want. It seems so unreasonable to be discontented.

I do not require you to be reasonable all the time. But I do appreciate your repentance. Start looking for what I am doing rather than lamenting what you are not doing. Gratitude is not difficult for you. I do hold you close. Feel My love. It has never vanished. I have never left you. Neither will I ever leave. Neither will I let you stray. I dwell in you, and you dwell in Me. It is not just a request or a wish, but a reality.

For so long, you have been asking, and wanting, sometimes wishing, even demanding union with Me. As it is happening, you don't quite know how to adjust. You need to be reminded that you already have what you truly desire. This is that living water. You thirst because you forget to drink. It is right there. Drink up.

Lord, how is it that when I expect You to be upset with me, You always just show me more love?

To quote the Bible, "God is love."

And I am delighted to receive.

By receiving, you also give love. I am delighted to receive your love.

Lord, You make repentance so much nicer than I ever thought of it. I come to You with a failing, and You bring victory from it. Thank You.

It is what I do. Penitence does not need to be distasteful. I am not anxious to burden those I love with remorse and heaviness. I simply want that you have life and have it more abundantly. I am not interested in punishment, but rather in positive change. Purification does not have to be painful. Remember My kindness and gentleness. I get accused of heavy-handedness, but that is not My way of doing things.

Your enemy wants you to be afraid. I tell you to "fear not." Yes, there is such a thing as "fear of the Lord," but the translation is faulty. That kind of fear is one of awe and wonder, not a cringing and worrying of what I will do to you if I should be displeased.

This is why I seem to be so slow to bring My justice to the problems of your world. You think I should punish or wipe out the ones who are causing all the problems in your country. You are waiting for disaster to hit them. Yet they continue to corrupt society. I work in ways you do not see.

When Saul was confronted, there is no record of his feeling bad about what he had done before his conversion, he was willing to turn his life completely around. *(Acts 9:1-22)* **It was not his blindness that did it, but My love. The blindness simply got his attention. I had much for him to do for Me. And he gladly did it all.**

Learn from the people in Scripture. Mary Magdalene was also turned around by My love, not My wrath. Come to My loving arms and when you find you have failed, be ready to do things differently, but without the fear. My love for you is a healing and transforming one. Yes, you are being transformed. It is working.

There was another thought that came to me that You might want to explain to me. The words were: active love and passive love.

Yes, I did want to talk to you about that. What do you think these terms mean?

I suppose active love is the kind that is felt. Like hugs and kisses and loving words and such. Passive love is knowing the love is there simply without demonstration. Just doing what is needed to be done without making a big deal about it.

That is close enough. Back when your husband was with you, he was not very demonstrative about his love, but you knew he loved you and your sons because he supported and protected you. You enjoyed each other's company even when there were no actions or words that are associated with love. But there were occasions of special heart-warming actions or even thoughts that would qualify as active love. When these were not present, the love did not cease. It was there whether exhibited or not. And you loved him the same way. He knew you loved him, and you knew he loved you. It did not have to be spoken all the time.

Loving your God is similar. You do what you think He wants and at times you attempt to voice your love or desire to show it as if He were visible. He often gives you the feeling of His Presence, that is His active love. Church services can be active love on both sides. You come to Me, and I come to you. Often in your prayer

times there is both active and passive love. Both are needed in a good relationship.

In friendships, both are necessary. That is why there are special occasions like birthdays and Christmas, which are occasions for active love. But just enjoying each other's company is still love. It is good to be aware of being loved. Not being conscious of it does not mean it is not there. It is nice to hear that you are loved, but you can know it without being told.

Being secure in the love of someone means you do not doubt it even when there are no active demonstrations of it. Remember when you were told that after 20 years of sticking with you, you could be secure in your husband's love. You never doubted it after that. Even when there was strife between the two of you, you both knew the love was there.

You now need to be secure in your God's love, and in your love for God. When you were in your teens, you realized that you did not know how to love God. But now you do know. And you have chosen to do so. And you know your God has chosen to love you regardless of your worthiness or lack of it.

Lord, Your Presence just came over me. It is as if You just kissed me. Thank You. Perhaps my delight in feeling Your Presence is my way of kissing You. And having You hold me through the night, that, too, is active love. But your provision of all I need, that could be passive love. But active or passive, it is love. And I thank You.

And your daily life when you are not actively aware of Me, that is passive love as well. But it is still love. And I also delight in being loved.

Lord, I want to thank You that I am secure in Your love. Are You secure in my love, too?

I can answer with My Name. I AM. I also have the advantage of knowing the end from the beginning. But you are right to ask. Love works best when both parties are involved.

Lord, I don't have anything else to talk about, but am so aware of Your love and goodness. Would it be OK to go back to bed and just enjoy it?

Yes. No deep teaching today, just experiencing love. It is good.

Thank You Lord for heavenly language when earthly ones fail. I thank You that Psalm 23 seems to be happening. There is nothing I shall want. You have provided everything I need. Thank You.

Maggie, praise and thanksgiving are indeed prayer. You have felt that your prayer times have not been useful unless there is a new nugget or truth or knowledge that you can share with others. You are not limited to your usefulness. I do not only love you for how I can use you, but I simply love you. You do not love Me just for what I provide, you have learned to love just being with Me. Wrapping your covers around you as if they were My loving arms is indeed prayer. It is not words, not revealing anything new, not asking for anything, not doing anything special, but just loving and being loved. It is important. When I tell you to go back to bed, it is not that I am tired of your written prayers, but that I also enjoy wrapping My arms around you and having you feel My love. No, you cannot let feelings run your life, but neither do you need to ignore them. Especially the good ones. They are to be cherished.

This is where Martha needs to rest and Mary takes over?

It is. And I am so glad that you can take the "better part" as Mary did. Go back and rest in My arms. I enjoy such obedience.

Me, too.

One day, the Lord asked me to begin to find one or two minutes at a time to focus on and actually feel His love. I gladly agreed, but found it much more difficult to do it.

Now I need You to tell me what to talk about, as my mind just went blank.

I can work with an uncluttered mind. How about one of those two-minute sessions where you just allow yourself to "feel" My love. You have not remembered to do that lately. No, not a time of repentance, right now, just love and joy....

My mind was not as uncluttered as I thought.

Now you know why you have not done this in a while. It is not as easy as you might think. When you pause to focus on My love, many other thoughts come rushing in. Not because of any lack of faith or goodness on your part, nor any lack of anything on Mine, but simply because it is not a usual pattern of thought. It takes practice. But it is a practice I want you to keep working on. Repentance and thanksgiving are good, but they are things you "do" while feeling My love is not an action on your part. It is a time, brief as it is, of receiving. It is being still. It is allowing Me to refill your spirit. Not yet comfortable to you. Is it?

I am surprised how hard it was. Is that why I have such a hard time at Adoration?

It is. It is also why you had such a hard time in keeping a "Holy hour" in the chapel years ago. Being Mary is not as easy as people think.

Does it get better with practice?

No, not just practice, but cooperation. You cannot do it alone. You need Me to make it happen. Doing something out of obedience is not what is necessary. It is like typing was for you in high school. No matter how hard you tried to do it well, you could not, as it was not something you were used to doing. You did not practice on your own, and when it was time for doing it in class, it was almost impossible. It was not until you started typing your notes into the computer that your typing improved. Then it was a means to an end you desired. It was not the typing that was important but having your writings readable. And it was not something trivial that you were typing, but something important to you.

Here is where the analogy differs from being still in My Love. It is not something you have to do because you were told to do it. But it is not even something you do by yourself. Why did you not practice typing in high school?

I did not own a typewriter. I did not even think to ask my father to use his.

But when you did own a typewriter later in life, did you get better at typing?

No, it was not necessary for me at the time. Now I am confused. There seems to be an aspect of asking You for the grace to do something You have asked me to do. Yet it is not something I "do" but there is practice needed and it has to be important to me. It is not as easy as I thought it would be, and I have to cooperate with You.

All of that is true. The difference between typing and adoration is that your only part is the choosing to do it. The rest is My part. It is not an activity of the soul, not the mind, only initially the will, and not even the emotions. Though all three will be affected, it is in the spirit where the focus is. My Spirit and your spirit must come together. It is the union you so desire. You need to ask, seek, and knock. But that is only the first step. Then you have to be still to receive, find, and enter.

Now it seems to make a bit more sense. I'm not sure I have it completely yet, but something I will need a lot of help with. I am delighted to provide the help you need.

Thank You, Lord.

Lord, would it be better if I had a particular place to do the short one- or two-minute pauses with You? Like the chair in my bedroom?

No. You are trying to legalize and complicate something that is meant to be simple and pleasant. Don't make it a chore.

I do that. I think there are many things I have made into chores, and that is why I resist them.

Can you just relax and let Me love you?

Is it that simple?

It is. Stop searching for deep and terrible character flaws. Let Me keep the job of perfecting you. I can do it better than you can. My love for you is better than your love for yourself. I know I said that you need to love your neighbor as yourself, but when you don't love yourself very much, things get distorted. Perfection is a lovely goal, but very exhausting. Let Me perfect you. And let Me be the judge of how it is going. Now go and rest in My arms, and just relax. Let My love take over.

Thank You.

I thought maybe this would be a good time to come to You.

Maggie, any time is a good time to come to Me. But it is very good that you are committed to coming to Me every night, regardless of the exact time. You encounter Me in many other ways daily, and it pleases Me. All the other prayers are valuable. And agreeing in prayer with those you listen to, that is helpful. But you are still not satisfied. I have not complained. What is it that you desire?

Sometimes I wonder about that myself. I am tired and often in a lot of pain. You sustain me, but I feel distant from You even though I am doing good things. When I am not actively speaking with You, like now, I feel like I forget You altogether.

That is why you cannot rely on feelings. When you were married, did you always need to feel close to your husband? Did you not engage in activities that had nothing to do with him? Did that cause a distance between the two of you? Were you not completely married to him regardless of what else was going on in your life?

You are Mine. Totally and completely. I am yours. Totally and completely. Can you come closer to Me more often than you do? Of course. Both you and I are working on that. But don't forget that I am still working on you and teaching you and revealing Myself to you. You want the end product, but do not always like

the process. Perfection is not for this side of eternity. Aiming for it is good, but do not be discouraged, as there is much joy yet to come in the process of getting there. Let Me be in charge of your progress. I am quite capable of correcting your path when I see the need.

Part of the problem is that you think all has been going so well, that there is a difficult time ahead, and you are dreading that. It is like being afraid of the dentist. You learned not to do that. As long as there is no pain, do not anticipate it. When it comes, you will have the grace to deal with it. Enjoy My pleasure with you. Let Me wrap My arms around you and remind you of My great love for you. Relax in My arms. Allow yourself to feel My love and your love for Me. You do not doubt My love for you. I do not doubt your love for Me. It is good.

Thank You, Lord. I will delight to feel You envelop me in Your love. It is such a privilege to be able to do that.

I thank You for the fact that I was sleeping very comfortably. But I refuse to be robbed of my time with You. Tonight, I will have a chance to practice what You told me yesterday. We have Adoration in the evening, and perhaps I can try being still in Your Presence. I only tried it once during the day, and it was not terrific, but You keep telling me not to grade my times with You.

Do you know why I tell you that?

I suppose because You see more than I do, and You want to encourage me.

Also, because I make use of even your feeble attempts and build on them. When you consider them unacceptable, how likely are you to keep at it? Then what do I have to build on?

But I want to offer You better things.

When one is learning to play a musical instrument, does it always sound wonderful at the beginning? Remember when your son tried the French Horn? At first it sounded like a dying moose.

But he got better, and eventually could play quite well. Yet he did not keep at it because he enjoyed the piano more.

It is all right to have a preference in types of prayer. But it is also good to be proficient at more than one way of communicating with Me. You speak more than one language. The different forms of prayer are like different musical instruments or different languages. Knowing more than one enhances your life and that of others as well. It gives you freedom to communicate better in different situations. But you will have your favorite, and the one you are most proficient at. The one you practice the most will be most comfortable. But you can rejoice in the opportunities I provide to use others.

Believe it or not, everyone speaks more than one language. There are languages most people speak, but do not even recognize that they do. There is body language. It is often better understood than most people realize. There is a language of caring and love. It need not be spoken, but often better understood than words.

Then there is the language of the Spirit. So it is with prayer. Mass is one language. Adoration is another. Coming to Me at night is still a different one and praying in tongues is still another. There are memorized prayers that come in handy at certain times and praying with others can take many forms.

Perhaps it is forms of communication that I am speaking of rather than languages. All are needed, even if they are not yet perfected. Sometimes you may not be proficient at one form of relating to others, but you can understand it. Children that grow up in households where another language is spoken can often understand much more than they can speak.

You are now exposed to prophetic prayer. It involves decrees, and taking authority, and things you were not exposed to before. But you are learning and can understand, though you do not necessarily use such ways of prayer yet. The dreams and visions others have, are also forms of communication. Dialogue is between at least two parties. I am one of those parties. Prayer in any form is reaching Me. And I have many ways to speak with you. Find Me in the forms that are not as familiar to you. You will be surprised how much you can understand. And if you don't understand, you can always ask for interpretation. Ask, seek, knock. It is all good.

Thank You, Lord. I needed that. Now I am looking forward to another form of interaction You and I have. When I get under the covers, I ask that You wrap Your arms around me as I rest. And You do. It is so good.

I did have an interesting dream. I think it was because I listened for the second time to one of my favorite ministers on YouTube talking about authority and power. In the dream, a large snake was attacking me, and I simply declared, "Satan, begone!" And it turned around and quickly slithered away. Both I and the person with me, were amazed that the authority worked.

The teaching in that dream is not that there was an attack, but that the authority does work and that it is amazing to even My own people. There is a partial belief, and a partial fear of presumption. It is all a part of not knowing Me well enough. You need to spend enough time with Me to know when and how to fight. As you continue to come to Me and I continue to instruct you, you will begin to know when and how I want you to act.

I do want an army of well-trained warriors. But the training is prayer. This is why I spent three years living and working with my apostles and disciples. It is only in living together that you can sense without instruction what your leader wants. That is why I spent much time alone with My Father. And I said I only do what He is doing.

Even though I lived with them, they bumbled a lot. But after I left, and the Holy Spirit empowered them, they were transformed into ones who changed the world. You, on the other hand, received the power of the Holy Spirit before you knew Me very well. All the power and authority were unused, because you did not know Me enough to understand how and when it is to be handled. You are now getting the training. As I pour out My

Spirit more abundantly, you will see and do things that did not seem possible before.

It is all for the glory of My Father. He is the compassionate One Who desires healing, and knowledge, and care of His children. Your motives have to be pure. I am purifying them. As you get to know and understand Me better, you will begin to conform to My desires and will be able to use the authority and power you have already received. You already have what I wanted My disciples to have.

You are delighted to belong to Me. That is what I told them. Do not rejoice in what you can now do, but rejoice that your names are in the book of Life, or in other words, you belong to Me. With Me all things are possible. Out of the relationship will flow the gifts.

In the past, you were more interested in the gifts than the relationship. That is why they did not work well. Now you are seeking the relationship, and whether or not you have the gifts is not as important. It is good. Now let My love enfold you and be assured that I am guiding you.

Lord, I thank You for my family. It was so good to spend quality time with them.

Maggie, it is good that you enjoy your family. I also enjoy My family. That includes you. Family is meant to be enjoyable. It is sin and evil that causes families not to be able to enjoy each other's company. It is the Father's plan and joy to see families that truly love one another.

Lord, I found a great freedom in just being able to see how the kids have matured. That they are handling their lives well and have not totally abandoned their faith. Please keep revealing Yourself to them and help them come closer to You.

Lord, I have also felt Your peace in my conversations with each of my family members. It is good to be at the age when I am not in a position to approve or disapprove of any part of their lives. I can simply listen and encourage and enjoy being with them. No control issues. It is refreshing.

See, old age does have some benefits. This is why I keep telling you not to grade or assess or judge everything, even your own progress. This is why you have enjoyed tutoring so much better than classroom teaching. You do not have to give grades. Your job is simply to help your students along, and someone else can do the assessment. You are now in that position with many members of your family. It is good not to need to be in control. You find that you do not even want to be in charge.

It is like performing in a play. You are not the director, neither are you just a spectator, but still an important part of the production. You have your role, are content with it, and perform it well. You need not be the main character, nor even desire to be. There is peace in knowing your part and doing it well. The striving is no longer necessary. It is good.

Thank You, Lord. It is indeed.

A few years ago, one of my grand-nephews suggested that we should have a family celebration to explain to the younger generation about our escape from Hungary. It was close to the American Thanksgiving time as we left Hungary on November 20, 1956, and arrived across the border in Austria to freedom on Nov. 23. We now call it a Hungarian Thanksgiving, and serve Hungarian food, decorate with Hungarian symbols, and present the story of our escape and the reasons we left. As I was preparing for this party of about 25 people at my house, I needed the Lord's help.

Here I am, Lord, ever so grateful for Your love and guidance.

Maggie, My love for you is so much greater than you can feel, know, or understand yet. I am guiding you and will continue to do so. Keep seeking My still small voice in the midst of all the activity this week. I will give you all the strength and help you need. It is good that you have begun the preparations. I am in this party you are having on Saturday. Do it all for Me.

Thank You, Lord, for reminding me. I need to do things for You, rather than because it is expected of me or just because I should. I tend to forget that. I offer everything to You each day, but then I seem to switch to "auto-pilot" and miss Your direction and purpose. Doing things for You, is so much better than just doing them. Love makes even difficult tasks delightful and easier. Help me to remember that it is all for You. Not that You need anything from me, but that it can be an expression of my love for You.

I need more ways to express my love for You. I now feel the difference between just doing things and doing the same things out of love. How is it that we miss this?

You have an enemy that does not want you to enjoy your service to Me. But I have defeated him, and you also have My authority to send him packing. Today, begin to be aware of all the things you do for Me. Just because the same things also benefit others, is a bonus. But let the motive be primarily that you are doing it for Me. This will lighten every task.

Thank You, Lord. I needed that.

I will need Your instructions as to whether I should stay home the morning before the party or if I should go to church as I usually do. If everything can be done today, I would prefer to go.

Lord, right now, I need to hear Your voice. My mind is too occupied with Martha things. So much needs to be done, and I had hoped that some of it would already be accomplished, but after all the shopping, I was too tired to start cooking.

And you want to put Martha to sleep for a while, and let Mary come forth?

Exactly.

I can help with that. Let's let Martha alone, and examine what Mary was doing. She sat at My feet, and listened to Me, and loved Me. She wanted to learn from Me. What did she call Me at the tomb when she realized that I was alive there? Rabboni. That means teacher. Her focus was on learning whatever I had

to say. Paying attention to someone is a "better part" than being busy serving. So, yes, come to church on Saturday, and leave the serving to others. Prepare as much as you can today. And let the rest go. It will all work out. Then when company comes, be ready to welcome them all, and enjoy each one. I Will be with you and delighted with it all. My love will show through. Be at peace.

Thank You, Lord. I feel Your Presence now and think I can sleep some more now. Funny how I was not even recognizing that I was full of worry, but that is what You told Martha, that she was worried about many things. I have been worried about many things, too. Help me to rely on You and learn from You, instead of worrying. Yes, I have a lot to do, but I am not alone. You can provide all I need.

See, it will all work out. Rest now.

Dear Jesus, thank You so much for all the joys and helps of yesterday. As You told me, everything is working out. My sister made one of the main dishes, I made another. She made the appetizer spread to put on crackers and I made bejgli *a nut roll for dessert)*. My bread machine was recently repaired by my niece's husband, and I have one batch of rolls made and will make another today. A friend from church brought cabbage noodles and cucumber salad. My grand-niece is making another meat dish, and nokedli *Hungarian noodles or spaetzles)*, and my grand-nephew who lives in another state is here and stopped by to say hello. I was able to get to church and our small group meeting, and will be at Mass again today. I think all I have to do today is the rolls and some creamed spinach, perhaps Mashed potatoes, but I'm not sure of that. Leah, my friend who helps me clean, was here and the house is clean enough, and I need to put the sofa cover in the dryer. Yes, I do sound a bit Martha-ish, but my heart is full of gratitude, and I am so glad.

You are a major part of this.

Maggie, I am a part of this. And I am glad you are working at the Mary aspect. Be at peace. All will go well, and I will give you the grace and the words for the story part. This is a good

thing. Enjoy all the company, and all the activity. Then let Me know what you think about it all. Go back to sleep for a bit now and let Me hold on to you.

Thank You so much, Lord.

Dear Jesus, thank You so much that the party went well. We had about 25 people here, and the food was plentiful, and everyone seemed to have a good time. We told our story of escaping from Hungary, and gave You glory and thanksgiving for all You have done for us. There are still dishes to be done, and many clean ones to put away, but that will be done today. Julie and Paul, my niece and her husband, were a tremendous help, and by the end of the day we were all exhausted. But it was well worth it.

Thank You so much, Lord.

Lord, I need to give You back all the controls. Thank You that my overbearing nature did not get past the thought level. I realized that I should not plan other people's schedules and am glad I did not say anything. I did not have much chance to speak with two of my grand-nephews, and I may not see them before they leave. But it was good to see them at all, so thank You for that.

Maggie, it all worked out, and you are learning that you need to let others run their own lives. You see how hard it is for Me to watch when My people do not do things. I wish they would. Like spending time with Me. Just as you wish they would have spent some of their time with you. I wish My family would come and spend more time with Me. But I have to let them come of their own accord. I do not nag or force them.

This is how I worked with you for years. I encouraged you to come to Me often, but if you did not, I waited until you did. See, here is another way you are becoming like Me. I am guiding you. This is also a part of aging gracefully. You realize that you no

longer are in the position of directing other people's lives. They have to follow their own path, and even if your thoughts or plans would benefit them, it is no longer your job to guide them. You can encourage and build up, or be there if they need to be consoled, but they have to take charge of their own lives.

It is a different part of love. You are no longer the caretaker, just the cheerleader. You need to shift gears and focus on learning what I want. Once again, remember all the times I went off to spend time with My Father? I needed His guidance as you also do. I said I only do what I see the Father doing. You need to see what I am doing and do likewise. It is a different way of seeing. Your physical vision may not be working well, but your spiritual vision can get better and better.

Let's work on that. Start looking for what I am doing. Soon you will also see what I want you to do, or not do. And realize that I am delighted to help you in this. I long for the opportunity to teach and guide you to see and do My Father's Will.

Lord, thank You. It is so good to think that I can please You. Please keep teaching me. And help me to realize that You are doing exactly that. Teaching me. I believe I am once again finding a love of learning.

Lord, I would like to listen to what is on Your mind.

First of all, I am delighted to be asked. I have many things on My mind, but mainly My love is the motivating force for Me. That is what I want My people to see and learn. Love is given and received in many ways. But it can be easily misunderstood. That is why I look at the heart, not just the actions. I see much more than you can. That is why you are not to evaluate or judge what you cannot possibly see. But your job is to love, and to receive love when it is presented to you. Gratitude is wonderful. It, too, is a gift.

Lord, let me express my gratitude to You. Thank You for all the gifts You shower on me every day. Help me to find ways to give You more gifts.

What you do for others, you do for Me. Rest in that.

Lord Jesus, how was Your Birthday?

It was good. The message of My love went out in many ways.

Lord, I felt like a little kid who wanted to give a gift to his parents, so he got them a toy truck. The parents graciously accepted it and saw the desire to please and to give. I wanted to spend these last two days enveloped in Your Presence, but what I felt was that I was trying too hard and feeling very little closeness to You. I wanted to give You something I thought You wanted, but actually tried to give You what I wanted.

Did I complain?

No, You seemed more amused at my feeble efforts.

But you gave Me a gift, and I accepted it. My love for you cannot be greater or less than total. And your love for Me is not measured by what you choose to give Me.

Am I still trying to measure love? And trying to control things?

That seems to be a tendency.

So how can I stop it?

By relaxing and letting Me take charge. Do not fear that you are not doing enough. Do not be constantly measuring yourself. It is like a child who wants to get taller, and is constantly checking his height, and disappointed that he had not grown any in one hour. Neither love nor holiness can be measured that way. It is a natural consequence of relationship. The relationship is alive and well. It needs no prodding. I simply love you. You know that and appreciate it. You also love Me. I know you will do anything I ask of you. But sometimes all I ask seems too insignificant to you. You want to do great things for Me. Great things are simply little things that fit together well.

Your book came about through a lot of little efforts. And when you thought it was all finished, there was still more to do with it. Even now, you are trying to figure out how to get it in the right people's hands. You are not finished with it yet. Neither am I finished with you.

Lord, I feel quite foolish, but grateful. Your patience and love are so much greater than I can comprehend. My desire is still total union with You. I am beginning to see that I do not have the concept of what that means. Even after all these years. You put that desire in me, and I believe it is also Your desire. And I do see some progress.

It is not up to you to measure that progress. Even what looks like total failure from your perspective, can be great progress in My sight.

I now understand a little about my blindness. I am not totally blind but am severely impaired in my sight. Apparently, it is not just the physical sight, but also the spiritual.

But though one deteriorates, the other is getting clearer. I can heal both. Let Me take charge. You cannot improve your eyesight by any effort on your part. If I see a need to heal it, I can do that. If I can teach you more by allowing it to continue, it is for your benefit. I did not heal every blind person in Israel. I did not cure every disease. But My love was withheld from no-one. I did not raise everyone who died. My supernatural actions have reasons that are not obvious to all. Many misinterpreted them. Many tried to manipulate them. But I reveal My reasons as I deem necessary.

Asking is not wrong. But there is the motive behind asking that can be. Zechariah asked in disbelief. Mary asked for understanding. Herod wanted to see a sign but never did. The disciples saw many. I look at hearts and motives. I respond as needed. Trust Me. I do all out of love.

Lord, I keep asking You to reveal Yourself to me in Your own way, and that is what You are doing. Thank You. I am in awe. Today is our family celebration of Your Birth. Please be with us. And help me to stop thinking I should be in charge.

Request granted.

Thank You also for the smile. Now please hold me through the rest of this night.

That request is also granted.

Dear Jesus, thank You that I slept well.

Did you feel My pleasure when you got up this morning?

I did, Lord. Thank You. I knew all was well. Then this morning, all I could think of was Your Father speaking at Your Baptism, that He was well-pleased in You. I felt like You were telling me that You are well-pleased with me. Somehow You have managed to clean me up from the inner turmoil of the past few days.

You seldom actually feel this grace, as life gets too busy. But you had a day of quiet service, and then some solid rest, and now you can see and feel your Father's love and pleasure.

I think I have felt it before, but seldom if ever, stopped to recognize it. Thank You for pointing it out. We get so caught up in trying not to displease Him, that we don't recognize His pleasure.

Is it a wonder that so many turn away from a God they think is always angry with them? So few understand complete love. They get glimpses of it at times but are too busy or distracted to savor those moments. I finally have you calm enough to see and feel the glory and beauty of being loved by your God. It is not just warm, fuzzy feelings. There is a peace and joy and a contentment that is shared between you and any or all Persons of the Trinity. But it is not only you who feel this, but you provide the same joy and peace and contentment to your God.

You are not used to thinking about God's feelings. When you have a child that does something good or loving, how do you feel? You are made in the image and likeness of God. Whatever you can feel, so can He. It is good that you finally can see this. Would that many others could also see.

And You are telling this to someone who is mostly blind.

There are different kinds of blindness. But that is a lesson for another time. For now, just be delighted that you see what you do.

That seems like a good plan. Thank You.

Lord, I thank You for all the ways You are teaching us. And thank You for a teachable heart, that we are still delighted to learn, especially to learn of You. We need to learn as we have had such awful misconceptions of You. You are revealing Yourself and Your love to us in marvelous and surprising ways. You are certainly answering my preparatory prayer I say each time I come to You in the night.

I do answer your prayers. I have answered your prayers all your life, but now you are more aware because you are paying attention and getting to know Me much better. This is relationship rather than servitude.

You have always loved serving Me, but now you love Me. There is quite a difference. I am not just a benevolent boss to you any longer. I am now immediate family. It is what I have desired, and I also put this desire in your heart many years ago. This is why you demanded union with Me when you did not think it was proper to demand anything of Me.

I have not changed, but your perception of Me really needed to change. And there is much more. I will continue to reveal Myself to you as long as you desire it and remain open and listening. It is a joy to My heart to have such a relationship with you, and not just you, but also those who will benefit from your writing these things down. My family is growing. It is the desire of My heart.

Lord, I love to know Your heart. It always surprises me how Your heart is so similar to ours. But then we were created in Your Image and Likeness, yet we are so amazed when we discover how much You are like anything that is good in us. Your gentleness and care overwhelm me. I am so blessed to come to know You this way.

Thank You for the past year. Please continue to help us through this new one.

I have no plans to leave you. I do have plans for your welfare and good. Continue to rely on and trust Me. You are firmly in My hands. You have learned to rely on Me much more than you ever had before. You managed not to worry through this past month. Keep focusing on My love, joy, and peace. The other fruits of the Spirit will follow naturally. New beginnings are My gift to you. A new Year offers new hope and new opportunities. It is good.

Lord, thank You for all Your gifts, graces, and blessings. Not only is this a new year, but a new week, a new month, and somehow a new energy. It is a good end of the year, and a good beginning of the new one. I don't know if I have ever felt this before. I believe You have given me one of those attitude transplants. I am not looking at the darkness, but Your Light. It is truly refreshing and unexpected. Thank You.

You are most welcome. I am delighted when you suddenly realize I have given you a gift. I am also delighted with your gifts to Me. Just accepting My love, joy, and peace is a gift you give to Me. Your awe and wonder warm My heart. Your desire to spread it to others is also your gift to Me. My love for you and your love for Me are continual gifts to be enjoyed and reveled in. Not just for you, but also for Me. I can also be caught up in awe and wonder.

Wow! I never thought of You that way. But it really makes sense. Thank You for revealing Yourself to me in another new way.

See, you are getting to know Me better. Was that not one of the parts of your prayer? I do answer prayers. Keep praying. We can both be delighted.

I now think all the festivities of the Christmas and New Year's season are finished. Thank You that everything that needed to be done was accomplished, and with much less stress than in past years.

It is sort-of another new beginning.

I see. What sort of a beginning is it?

What would you like it to be?

Actually, I need to know what <u>You</u> would like it to be.

How about taking one day, one moment, at a time and discovering it together?

That sounds quite reasonable.

I'm glad you approve.

Lord, You are making me smile again.

I know. I have to have some fun once in a while, too.

Let's have some fun together in this new beginning.

That is quite possible. It is a much better plan than most New Year's resolutions.

Lord, I love You.

Now that is a good beginning. I also love you. Love can be great fun at times. It is worth exploring. Now rest in My loving arms. We will explore in the morning.

Thank You, Lord.

After telling the Lord of several incidents through the day

Having trouble connecting with Me?

Yes, I seem to be rambling, not quite knowing how to start.

Start with My love. Relax a bit. I have not changed.

Lord, yesterday I recognized a loneliness in someone. I used to feel the same way when I was in high school. She desperately needs the friendship only You can provide. Yet we keep on looking for it in others and are repeatedly disappointed. But it was so hard for me to rely on You for such friendship and love, and even now, I seek it from others. If You give me a chance to talk to her about it, please be with me and give me the best words to help her.

Now you see why you were having difficulty praying tonight. This was for her. You were able to identify a problem she is having, by feeling a similar situation from your past.

I see it now. Thank You. It may take me a while to process this. But suddenly I feel connected to You again, and deeply grateful.

It is good. The processing will happen through the day.

The next day:

Thank You for allowing me to help another friend with loneliness. I hope it helps her and will offer her some diversion. You worked in an amazing way. You alerted me to one person's loneliness, and then helped me minister to someone else's. You are awesome!

I did kind-of sneak that one in, didn't I?

Yes, You did, and I am grateful. You reminded me of something a beloved priest said to me once during confession. I don't remember the context, but it must have been about some feelings, and he said that those were not for me, but for my ability to help others. I did not fully understand it then but was comforted by what he said.

Last night I was realizing that perhaps some of the emotions we experience are really not ours but given to us in order that we can understand someone else. I also remembered many more years ago, when I was totally desolate in my emotions, but stuffed then down so deep, that I had almost eradicated all emotion so I would not lose control. It was at a prayer meeting and someone else began to weep uncontrollably. She could not understand why she was weeping, as she was not upset, but I instinctively knew that she was expressing what I could not. The feelings she was exhibiting were mine. I believe You allowed her to express what was inside of me so it could be brought to the surface and healed.

In the healing ministry, we often feel a pain that is not our own, as You show us that someone is being healed of whatever we are feeling. Is it that way with emotions, too?

It is, but I don't want you to go overboard with this. Just as not every pain you experience is a healing of someone else, nether

is every emotion you feel there for others. Just because I can use you this way, does not mean that I will do it all the time or even often. You cannot live your life unsure of reality. Remember that I usually choose to work through natural means. Supernatural healing of both bodies and emotions is not the ordinary way I do things. If you are looking for these experiences, they will quickly become fake and ineffective. You have to live your life in the natural and allow Me to use you supernaturally when I choose to do so. When I do, it will only be seen after the fact. If you keep your focus on Me, instead of the gift, for this is indeed a gift, then I will work it all out. As soon as you think you are in control, it all falls apart.

I see it now. Thank You for the warning. Use me this way when You want to, and I will gladly be surprised when You do.

I am here at Your service, listening for Your voice. I am concerned for my friend who is distressed with her memory loss.

I am happy to answer. The ministry you are providing for your friend is training for you and for anyone she calls. Whether or not it helps her, it is helping you. As long as you do it out of love and care, it does help her for a while. But the training for you is to be willing to do it without expecting or even knowing if it is at all effective. You have to speak to her as unto Me. As long as you do it to My sister, you are doing it for Me. Right now, she is going through her "Agony in the Garden". Pray with her, for her, and listen. I will guide you. I do love her and she does know and love Me. Keep reminding her of that. And remember that as you dispense My love to her, some of it settles on you as well. Each time I use you in this way, My love in you grows. Cherish that growth. And do that with anyone who comes to you whom you can love, care for, or encourage. I am at work in you. You are the channel of My love.

Thank You, Lord. I will pass this message on.

Good. I am with you.

Lord, last night I thoroughly enjoyed a hot fudge sundae, and did not have any ill effects. Lord, it is good to be able to truly enjoy something like that and not feel I am being sinful for liking it so much. With all Your goodness, how did we get to the point of thinking that any enjoyment is wrong?

It is because the carnal nature has a tendency to over-indulge and what would be good on occasion, becomes an addiction.

That makes sense, and I have lived that. I used to think moderation was unattainable for me. But You have calmed many of my excesses. Now I wonder if it is possible for me to enjoy spiritual things as much as I enjoyed that hot fudge last night. I want my love for You to be stronger than my love for things

I want that as well. But it does not mean that you cannot ever have the things your body or mind or senses enjoy. Remember what a former spiritual director told you about his experience as a novice. His devotion to Me prompted him to tell his spiritual director that he wanted to give up everything he enjoyed in life. His director quickly answered, "You will go crazy in two weeks if you do that."

I have filled this world with good and enjoyable gifts. There is a balance between self-denial and self-indulgence. You learn how great it is to love by being loved. You want to give gifts to others that they enjoy. I also like to give gifts to you that you enjoy. But I will not have you eat hot fudge sundaes on a daily basis. There is a balance. Both sides of the balance are My love for you.

The proper response is gratitude? Both for the gift as well as for the limits on it?

Yes, and no. Gratitude is wonderful, but it is to be genuine, and not forced or overdone. Sometimes pure enjoyment is gratitude in itself. I love to see happiness. You do, too. You don't want to be around people that are habitually unhappy. Neither do I.

Yet many think that all I want is sacrifice or pain. I heal. I teach how to be truly happy. Look at the beatitudes from a different point of view. Why are the poor in spirit blessed? It is not their poverty, but their attitude that even in poverty there are joys and blessings. Why is mourning blessed? Because there is love behind mourning, and the comfort that will come once the pain ceases in remembering that love.

When I recounted my Lenten plans, the Lord replied.

It looks like it will be an interesting Lent. I have provided all you need, except constant reliance on Me. That you will have to do. But I will continue to lavish you with love, joy, and peace.

At that point, my mind went blank, and I did not know how to continue.

Now that we have had discussion, and you are not upset that there was nothing to say, it is time to allow Me to love you. No words necessary, just accepting and receiving and gratitude is a returning of My love that is pleasing to your God.

Not just one-way. Remember the waves of water at the river? And the ripples that return to the river? Here, the ripples are not loving others, but acceptance, reception, and gratitude are the return I desire. Praise and worship also happen as a result.

Lord, Your goodness seems to be washing over me. I feel like I don't have to do anything at all, You are doing everything. Thank You.

On Good Friday, I first recounted all the events in my life at that time:

That is my life, but the most important part of these days is Yours. I have a difficulty with time. I know all that we are commemorating happened a long time ago, and knowing how it did turn out with Your Resurrection, it is hard for me to be fully engaged in the liturgies. I go, and participate as best I can, but to me, You are alive even on this day of the year.

Remember when you saw a documentary about the Hungarian revolution many years ago, and heard how the new leaders were asking for world help? You became emotional because you knew there was to be no help coming. My life is similar, but in reverse. You hear about the distress and cruelty but know that redemption and Resurrection is the result. Though my death is commemorated today, I AM alive. Your love for me is not determined by your emotions or lack of them. Neither is My love for you.

Thank You, Lord. Please help me get through this day.

As the family gathers to celebrate Your Resurrection, please come and be with us, and help us to not only enjoy the food and the company, but to include You and honor You.

It is good that Lent was fruitful, and it is also good that its end is here. It is time for rejoicing. As you rejoice, so do I. My mission was finished on the Cross. Your mission continues, but with greater assurance of My love, care, and help. The curtain is torn, and you have free access to your God. I did rebuild the temple in three days. You are also that temple. My Presence within you is indeed glorious. You have full access to the Father, to Me, and My Holy Spirit.

Every year as you go through Lent and My passion and death and Resurrection, all is renewed, and you can get even closer than before. I died once for all, but there is power to be had through the remembrance. It is power you need. I am delighted to provide it. Remember how much I love you.

One night I just went on and on relating the events of the day

Lord, I seem to be babbling, as if trying to distract You from whatever You may want to bring to my attention. Sorry. I am listening now.

Actually, you are simply inviting Me into whatever is on your mind. It is good. It is what friends do. You have been wondering if you need to pay more attention to My Father and Holy Spirit. Many years ago, you learned that speaking to any One of the Trinity does not exclude the other Two. But you have felt the need for Fathering and have not specifically addressed Our Father in private prayer in a while. Neither have you prayed in the Spirit on your own recently. And you are feeling these needs.

This is your need, not an offense against your God. Remember that all Three Persons of the Trinity are pleased with your devotion and love. But it is the comfort and reassurance of the Spirit that would soothe your soul, or the loving embrace of the Father that you long for. When you address Me, you have the attention of the One God, in all Three Persons. But your focus is limited, and you are not aware of the workings of all Three Persons. I promise not to feel neglected if you spend time in the Father's arms or enveloped in the Spirit's embrace.

Just because you address Me in your prayers, does not separate Me from the Father or the Spirit. It is easier for you to imagine Me, as I took on human form. You know I had arms that could hold you. You do not know exactly how to picture either the Father or the Holy Spirit. But you experience the love and care and provision you receive. Right now, you are aware of My (plural) Presence. It is good. Now that you are more aware of all Three Persons' love and care, you can go back to bed assured that all is well. My arms, the Father's arms, and the Holy Spirit's arms will all enfold you and you can sink into the comfort of the entire Trinity holding you.

Lord, I am overwhelmed and delighted. Thank You.

Come Holy Spirit, I seem to need help again.

That is good that you need help. I am delighted to give you all the help you need. Try looking up Psalm 100.

Yes, Lord, You are good, and Your faithfulness is for all generations. Last night I had the opportunity to interact with many little children. Their boundless energy and curiosity were delightful. Do You also take delight in such things?

Not only in the very young, but also in My people at all stages of life. I love life. I love goodness and kindness, and the awe and wonder you experienced just watching and interacting with those little ones. I experience awe and wonder, too.

You find this surprising. You thought that since I know everything, I am immune to ordinary feelings, especially good ones. No, it is not like that. I am within you. I feel all that you feel. Union is like that.

But I feel like it is not yet complete. I can believe that You can feel what I feel, though I had not considered it much before, but I don't think I feel what You feel yet. I remember being afraid of loving You for this reason. I worried that if I truly loved You, all the things that hurt You would hurt me as well.

You assured me that since there were good parts to love, that I would be able to handle it. Now that I no longer doubt my love for You, I wonder if I am capable of feeling what You feel.

This is why you are still learning. Keep watching and learning, and do not be afraid. Love works both ways, and it will be perfected.

Dear Jesus, I may get to see two of my sons today.

Maggie, just as you long to see your children, so I also long for them to come back to Me. Just as your arms ache to hold them once again, so My arms ache to hold them as well. Remember that in your intercessions. When you pray for the salvation of souls, it is My longing for them that you are uniting your prayers with. It is not trying to convince Me to bring them to Me but cooperating with Me to fulfill My heart's deepest desire.

Lord, I never thought of it that way. Thank You that You love them more than we ever could. And thank You for putting such love into our hearts as all love comes from You. The love I feel for all my sons is very strong. But Your love is perfect. You created each one. You watched and guarded them as they grew, and You long for them to be able to return that love to You. You have blessed me with sons who do return my love for them as best they can. Let me, at least be such a daughter to You, who not only appreciates Your love, but loves You to the best of my ability. Please increase my ability to love You.

That is exactly what I have been doing. Be at peace.

Lord, even though the weekend was turbulent at times, Your love and the love of my family was so great and evident. I thank You. I needed that.

I know. I will always meet your needs. The love is always there but is not always easy to see. Sometimes it is wrapped in turmoil, but the core is still love. It is how the world situation is right now as well. There is much turmoil and yet My love can be seen through it if one is aware of it. I gave you a great gift in opening your eyes to the love behind the turmoil this weekend. Now, you can see it as it is. Look for My love and the love of others under the surface. It is always there.

Thank You, Lord. I guess I am not as blind as I thought I was. This is all Your doing.

The day after my birthday:
Maggie, you knew I was with you through the whole day and was as delighted as you were. You may not have thanked me for each part of the day, but your attitude of gratefulness showed that you knew I was behind all the jewels of love that were showered upon you. You did hold My hand tightly and felt every blessing throughout the day.

This is abundant life. This is union. Not much out of the ordinary, but spectacular when put together. All the fruits of the Spirit came together in one day. You were filled with love, joy, and peace. Patience came in when you had bad directions to where you were going. Goodness and generosity came to you through others. Gentleness in the healing service after Mass with the laying on of hands, kindness and faithfulness through each phone call, and self-control in skipping dinner after a big lunch. The fruits work whether you are the one showing them or receiving them. You can eat a fruit or give it to someone. Either way, it is sweet.

Would You lead us in prayer as I will have a friend here this afternoon. It is the National Day of Prayer, and we will want to pray for our country, and it is better when two or more come together in agreement.

Yes. Pray as much as possible today in agreement with Me and all the prayers for the country. Continue in the joy and peace I provide. Do not let go of My hand. I continue to be with you at every step.

I am overwhelmed by Your love. And I thank You. It is so good to be in Your care. And being aware of it is truly wonderful.

Lord, I know there are many in the Church who know we need a revival, but so many do not seem to see it at all, including our leaders. Please let Your fire fall and bring the Catholic Church into agreement with the Pentecostal and evangelical parts that we may be one as You and the Father and the Holy Spirit are One. Bring signs and wonders into our services, and let Your people experience Your power and healing. We certainly need that.

I am working to do exactly that. I know when you hear of things that encourage you, you expect to turn on the news and hear that it has happened. Then you are disappointed when there is no such news. I work behind the scenes. Trust Me. None of your prayers or those of those who agree with you will go to waste. I

am showering the world with faith. But remember how your faith took time to grow even after you chose to believe.

The seeds have been sown. Give them time to grow. Just as your figs are growing and ripening, it makes no sense to pick them until they are ripe. They will ripen if you let them stay on the bush a bit longer. Trust Me. I know the right time for harvest. Soon does not mean this minute. But soon does not mean years either. Keep listening and praying. Be ready for My use. But do not rush ahead of My directions and pick unripened fruit.

You have begun to consult Me before you jump into action hoping it is My Will. Keep doing that. I will ask things of you that you longed to do and are now ready to do them. Like your pastor asking you to pray for a family. He gave you no details, but you were delighted to be asked. And now you are doing exactly what you have been asked to do. This is ministry. You have longed for ministry, and now you are ready for this one. Enjoy the pleasure of your God.

See, here is another way you have found to please God. And you are beaming at the thought. And My presence is upon you. Isaiah 43 is happening. "Fear not, for I have redeemed you, I have called you by name, you are Mine.

Lord it is so good to be Yours. So many times I have felt that I did not belong wherever I found myself, and worked really hard to fit in. Belonging is a wonderful gift to me. I thank You that You will never reject me. I truly belong to You. I have had a lot of practice with rejection. But belonging to You heals all that. Thank You.

Not only do you belong to Me, but My love surrounds you and enfolds you and cannot be taken from you. Belonging is good but being cherished and appreciated is even more fulfilling. I am your God. I belong to you as much as you belong to Me. But as your relationship with Me has grown, I feel cherished and appreciated by you. It delights Me. It is not a one-way street. Take the time to "feel" your God's pleasure.

How do you think I felt when I heard My Father say, "This is My beloved Son in Whom I am well pleased." It made Me desire to fulfill His plan for me even more than I was already committed to do so. It made it all possible. It carried me through the agonies I needed to suffer. Remember My humanity. I was affected by many things just as you are. Though I am Love, I am also moved by love. Your love is very precious to Me. It has grown and will continue to grow. I value it more than you can imagine.

Lord, You are revealing Yourself to me in ways I never imagined. Thank You. Please hold on to me.

I am delighted to do so.

Of course, our country and the world are in a great mess, but You know all that. Actually You know everything, but You told us to tell You things, here I am doing so.

Yes, it is good for you to tell Me things. And I tell you things as well. That is how relationships develop. It does not matter that I know the facts of which you speak, I delight in hearing how you perceive those facts. I like to hear your voice and thoughts. When you pray this way, without actually voicing anything, it still counts. This is essential communication.

There are other forms of connecting with Me beyond this. You have a relationship with your dog. It usually is not verbal, you do not type letters to her, but you do communicate. You know when she wants or needs things, she seems to know your ways, and it is a good relationship. There are many people in your life with whom you have a connection. Some very close, some not so close. But it is good and proper that they are different.

You have had some relationships that were not good and are glad they no longer plague you. Others were great but are over for various reasons. But your communion with Me is different. It has many of the same aspects as other contacts, but there are many parts that are greater and deeper than possible with everyone else. Omnipresence, Omniscience, and such things make a difference.

Love makes it all good. Because you love Me, you are glad I am always with you and never leave you. Because you love Me, you are also delighted that I know and understand you and every-

thing you bring to Me. Because you know that I love you, you know you can trust Me with anything. And this relationship will never end. Eternal life, when combined with love and trust is beyond wonderful. Both for you, and for Me.

Thank You, Lord. We tend to forget Your side of things. Yes, we want to please You, and avoid offending You, but how often do we actually try to consider what You think or feel? Yet You have been telling me these.

Help me to focus more on You than on me. You have allowed me to have relationships where I considered the other person's needs or wants or thoughts more important than mine because I loved them. Can I, and do I treat You like that? Help me to do so more consistently. Your invisibility does make it more difficult, but not impossible. Yes, You and I are both smiling. I keep complaining about Your invisibility, but You assure me that it is necessary. I have no choice but to accept that.

But just think of how great it will be on the other side of eternity when that will not be necessary.

I know. But I expect I will still complain about it on this side of eternity.

I can handle that. Now enjoy this day and this love as well as those others in your life.

Lord, You are so good to me. Thank You.

Lord, I want my time with You, here I am.

And so am I. You listened to the story of the Prodigal Son again yesterday and realized that I am teaching you pretty much what you are hearing. My Father is more interested in hugging you than He is in anything you do. And I only do what I see the Father doing. I delight in wrapping My arms around you each night.

Love is Who your God is. All three Persons. Love is likened to a fire, but this fire only has the positive qualities of fire. Moses saw a burning bush that was not destroyed by this fire. It pro-

duces heat, and light, and can cleanse, but it never destroys or hurts. That is why Elijah could get into a fiery chariot, and why the three young men in the furnace were not harmed. Man produces fire that has destructive aspects to it.

The fire of My love is only good. And the fire of this love is for you. Personally, for you. Yes, it is available to everyone, but when received, it becomes very personal and intimate. That is why when you see pictures of Pentecost, the fire is on each person individually. I can do that. And I want to do that. You do not need to beg for this fire of My love, it is why I came to earth. It is why I wanted this fire to be blazing. I still do.

As you learn more about My love, you can spread it to others. Gently, calmly, quietly, almost invisibly, you can join Me in spreading such love. And you do. Keep doing so. This, too, is part of union with Me. It is your heart's desire. And Mine as well.

Lord, I am in awe. Thank You ever so much.

After a powerful prayer meeting
Lord, I thank You that You came with great power and gentleness and love to help us with the big things, as well as the small, insignificant ones. You are awesome!

It is My delight to be with all of you. With so much love in that room, how could I not have ministered to each of you. Yes, My Spirit did flood this place and the atmosphere did become heavenly. Each of you is growing in intimacy with Me, the entire Trinity. You are fulfilling Scripture in finding how to please God.

You have each been Fathered, loved, guided and blessed. And your desire to return the Fathering by "Daughtering" is also very pleasing to the Father. Just as I often tell you to just pause and enjoy My peace and love, your God was able to pause and enjoy and relish the love each of you offered Him. He can say to each of you, "you are My beloved daughter, in whom I am well-pleased.

Lord, there is no way we can ever thank You. But we will continue to try. It is so good to belong to You.

Chapter 3

The Joy of the Lord is my strength

Every morning during your morning offering, You offer Me all your prayers, works, joys, and sufferings. But you think I only want your sufferings. Yes, I do use all the pains and troubles you offer Me as raw materials for a blessing either for you or someone else, but don't you think I can do that with the more positive aspects of your life? I want you to focus on the prayers, works, and joys more than just the sufferings. They are My gifts to you, and as You offer them back to Me, they become even more precious in My sight. And, yes, I can use them to fashion blessings as well.

I have a friend, Pattie, who comes to visit me for a few days every year for her birthday. When I first met her, she was having a lot of troubles, but over the years, the Lord worked wonders in her life and she is now doing well.

Lord, yesterday You encouraged me to pray more fervently for my friends, our priests and all ministers. I have been and will continue to do so. Some of the messages I listened to yesterday seem to confirm that this is exactly what I am to do. Thank You.

You did not know that this friendship you have with Pattie is really My Will for you. It has been from the beginning. Through

you in her life, I not only touch her, but all those she interacts with in her life. I have given you the joy and ability to teach her in ways others cannot. She, in turn, teaches others that would not be willing or able to learn from usual teachers. I am using you in ways you often do not see. And I am gifting you with such a joy while I am working through you.

The work you do for Me is infused with joy. Just as when you cared for your mother, you not only knew you were doing My Will, but you thoroughly enjoyed it. So, it is now. It is My gift to you, as well as your gift to Me. Both of you are delighted in My Presence. This is as it is meant to be. There is joy in it. Both for her, and for you.

Do you notice how so many things are two-way streets? You cannot connect with Me without both you and I being affected. I am as delighted in your presence as you are with Mine. Any good conversation or friendship is to benefit both parties. When you enjoy something good, others are also affected. If no-one else seems to be involved, there is always the cloud of witnesses that are rejoicing with you. I am involved with all of your life.

You offer yourself to Me daily, and I give Myself to you daily as well. But it is not only in times of personal or formal prayer that I am with you, but all the time. Begin to think on this. I know you are not aware of My Presence all the time yet, but that is a goal both for you and for Me. It is the union you so deeply desire. I, too, desire it. Our hearts are burning with this desire. Yes, the fire of My love has been kindled in your heart. I am so pleased that it is blazing. It is also touching others, and that, too, is My desire and Will.

No longer do you need to wonder if the things you do are part of My Will or not. You can have confidence that I am in the midst of your life and will continue to guide and direct you.

Lord, I am feeling this confidence, but wonder if I will become over-confident and mess up.

Am I not capable of correcting you when you make a mistake? You have seen that My corrections are loving and kind and gentle. I do not berate you. I teach and confirm you. Fear not! I have redeemed you, called you by name, and you are Mine.

I have always loved that quote from Isaiah 43. But before, I only hoped it applied to me. Now, I see it as reality. Thank You.

One day, a friend unexpectedly came over with her adult grandson, for whom I had been praying, and he helped me do several things I was not capable of doing myself.

You see I can surprise you with blessings you had not even imagined. It is good that you recognize that it was not just the kindness of a friend, but My gift to you. And you had a new appreciation for someone you have been praying for. He even seemed to enjoy the service he provided for you. My plans are like that. All are blessed. Each day can be an adventure of finding what blessings I have prepared for you. That is the abundant life. It is yours. I came that you can have it.

So many miss it because they are too focused on the negatives. Yes, there are problems, also, but I provide so much more good than My people realize. Even in great disasters like the recent hurricane, I send good and kind people to help.

How do you like My lessons on joy?

I really appreciate them. You have been changing my focus so I can see so much more of Your goodness, kindness and gentleness. You have always been that way, but I was so preoccupied with negatives that I allowed the world's misconceptions about You to rob me of much of Your gifts. Help me to keep remembering what you are now teaching me.

I am good at that, too.

Lord, You made me smile again. It is so good to be able to just have some fun with You.

A good relationship has to have an element of fun. It cannot just be fun all the time, but it is meant to be enjoyed by both parties. I can laugh and enjoy things just as you can. And I do. Yes, I deal with much trouble and pain as well, but I delight in the love

and joy of My family. And you are part of My family. Let that sink in. Not only are you part of My family, but unlike families, I have chosen you to be. Most people cannot choose their relatives. I created you because I wanted you in My family. I do not do things by chance.

Lord, I have much to think about, and it is all good. Thank You.

Thank You that my sister is here. It was so good just to sit and talk and both of us simply enjoying each other's company.

Lord, right now I am most grateful for the pure joy and comfort in which I slept tonight. There are so many nights when I simply can't get comfortable, either because of pain, or restlessness, or my mind refusing to shut down. Somehow, everything was perfect, and I had no pain, no cramping, was not too hot or too cold. Even my dreams were calm and gentle and pleasant. I would gladly have stayed there, as I understood that it was only because of Your great love and care that I was feeling so good and cozy. But I also knew that You meet me when I come to You at the computer. I can feel just as much of Your goodness, or even more, when I come to You in the dark of night.

It is good that you came out here to talk to Me. The same joy you felt last night being with your sister, is what I feel when you come to Me, especially when you choose to give up something you are really enjoying in order to spend time with Me this way. Yes, you can give Me joy. And you do it more often than you realize.

Lord, as I was on my way out here, I was thinking how I wish more people knew how wonderful it is to belong to You. To be enveloped in Your love and care and feel Your pleasure. And You reminded me that my writing can tell more people about it. That filled me with even more gratitude. That I can be of use to You this way.

And you were worried that your usefulness to Me would disappear due to your age and disabilities. I will never stop loving you or caring for you or allow you to become useless. I am the One who put the desire for usefulness within you. I also have that

same joy in serving My Father, and in turn serving all those I love, including you. Yes, I still serve. And I am delighted to do so. You are made in My image and likeness. That includes the delight in service and the delight in fellowship.

Just as you enjoy the company of your sister, or just about anyone else, so I also enjoy both your joy in those situations as well as, or even more, the times you come to be with just Me. Being alone with one you love is delightful. It is also wonderful to be with one you love in many other situations. But it is different.

That is why you have been confused about personal prayer versus corporate prayer. You do not feel My love the same way at Mass or at Benediction as you do when you are having conversations with me in the middle of the night. It is different. But both are good. You have been going to Mass and often having to work hard to get to do so since childhood. Whether or not you ever felt anything, you kept coming to Me that way. And I meet you there, but not in the same way I meet you here, in the privacy of our conversations.

I have given you both the joy of privacy and the joy of being with others. Some people are much more comfortable in private, while others crave the companionship of other people or even a lot of people around them. I have given you both these joys. I also had them both. I could go off to a lonely place to be alone with My Father, and also enjoy the company of any or all of My disciples or be delighted to speak to crowds as well.

You are sharing in My ability to enjoy all these situations. This is why I have been teaching you about joy. It is good to take and feel joy in many different ways. But being aware of the joy I hide in so many situations, that is a special gift you are discovering.

Now you need to go back to that warm bed and enjoy the little time left before the day begins. With that invisibility thing, I can be there with you just as easily as I can be here with you.

Lord, You make me smile again. Thank You.

Lord, my mind was running fast last night. I thought so much about the negativity of our culture and society, and how to combat that. I want to bombard as many people as possible with the positive aspects of life. Especially about having children. You create children to be a blessing, but we have believed the lie that they are a burden instead. I remember when I first realized that I had bought that lie. I wept in repentance. And You changed my perspective. My children have been a great blessing to me. I enjoyed motherhood and saw so many great and wonderful miracles You gave me through my children. If we would talk about those things more than complaining about the difficulties, we could help change this culture. Perhaps that is another reason You are having me write another book. Lord, keep me listening and writing what You want to tell Your people.

Yes, I do want My people to concentrate on what is good. See Philippians 4. The stories of the aged need to be about the good they have experienced. Not just their aches and pains. You can complain to Me, as I can handle it, but to the younger folks, they need to be built up with positive thoughts. I have a reason for making you an author at this age. I do have many things I want to show others. I want you to get them thinking in better ways, and they will also begin to hear Me.

The time of lamenting and mourning needs to be over, and joy must fill the earth. Joy will strengthen my people and shall be a great weapon against the evil in the world. Choose to be joyful. Choose to think about positive and beautiful things. I do not ask that you deny that there are things that are wrong or painful but push through them while concentrating on what is good.

Remember after a surgery on your shoulder, you suddenly realized that though the shoulder was painful to move, the elbow and fingers still worked. It made recovery easier. In the same way, there are still aspects of your life and world that are working and are good. Think on these things. I provide you with many gifts, graces, and blessings. Look for them and give thanks. Soon you will see that they truly outnumber the problems and pains.

Let My love and care become the most frequent of your conversations. Confirm to each person that they have a good purpose

for which I created them. That they are alive for such a time as this. That I purposefully made them and preserved their lives. Just as I did with you. I continue to prepare places for them right here on the earth as I also prepare a place for them in heaven.

This is the abundant life I want them to have. It does not necessarily mean riches as the world thinks of riches, but there are riches many miss as they are looking for what does not satisfy. Let the fire of My love be kindled and fanned into a blaze.

Wow, Lord, Your mission for me has become so much more urgent. Help me do exactly what You desire.

I received the formatted copy of my manuscript, Grace and Gratitude, and can make up to 100 corrections. I have gone through 40 pages so far and have two corrections ready. Please help me get through all of the book, and alert me to whatever needs to be fixed.

Lord, as I was listening to the computer read my book to me, it was as if You were once again talking to me as You did when I first wrote it down. Much of it still applies and I, myself, need to hear it again. I now see the truth in what one of my favorite teachers said, that as we remember the old stories, the power of that time returns and does what is now necessary. I really hope that others will be as encouraged by all You have said and done in my life as they read this book.

Maggie, it is true. You felt My Presence as you re-lived those times. Keep working on it until you can finish it, and then begin re-reading these current ones. There really is another book emerging, and I have plans to help many through it. But you cannot live in the past or the future. Both are good, but the present is My present for you. Open that present eagerly each day, and let's enjoy as much as possible, while enduring the difficulties.

You give yourself to Me completely, and I give Myself to you completely. The union you and I both desire is happening. Generally, it is not spectacular, but I do have some surprises still in the works. A deep abiding peace and joy is what I truly give

you and desire for you to have. And as you experience that, it will spill into others' lives as well. See how good My plans are?

I do indeed, and You again make me smile. I am so glad I belong to You.

So am I.

As I was wondering whether Grace and Gratitude *would actually help anyone, the Lord assured me:*

My Spirit is at work to bring My people's attention to what they need. The work you have done in writing it will bear fruit, but you may not see it in this life.

I see. I will leave the successes or failures in Your hands. I am glad You are using me to show people Your goodness. As I read through the book yesterday, I saw how You promised me that You would use me in ways I could not imagine. That is what You are doing by making me into an author. Thank You for such a ministry.

And a ministry it is. A long time ago, you asked Me for a ministry. Then I answered with the extraordinary Eucharistic ministry. You were delighted with that. Now I give you this ministry, and I see you are again delighted. That is very pleasing to your God.

Lord, how often You have told me that pleasing You is simpler than I expect. Simply enjoying Your gifts to us pleases You.

And so many think I am hard to please. I am delighted to reveal this to you and those who will read your writings. I told you many times that I am not finished with you yet.

And now I finally believe it. Thank You so much. It is such a privilege to serve You this way. It is not what I ever imagined I could do, but then I did very little of it. You are the One who did most of the work. Is healing the same way? We are simply a conduit for what You want to do, and we happen to be available to Your use?

Yes, most of the work I do is through My friends. Now you see one of the benefits of that invisibility thing. If I were visible, I would not need so many "conduits" to accomplish the Father's

Will. As it is, I can and do use so many, and the benefits are magnificent. The "conduits" are blessed, the recipients of my gifts are blessed, and My Father is pleased. This is the way it is supposed to work. When it does, it is glorious.

Thank You for allowing me to have a part in Your work. Being a "conduit" is a pretty great role. It makes submission and surrender desirable. I am getting a glimpse of how simply allowing You to do Your work through me, takes all the pressure off of me. The pressure is only when my own will is not submitted to Yours. I am in awe.

Just where I want you to be. It is an answer to the part of the Our Father. Thy Kingdom come; Thy Will be done. This is why the Kingdom of God is within you. You are its conduit. It is how His Will can be done, through all the conduits. Pretty cool plan, isn't it?

Yes, it is. I never expected it to make so much sense.

Lord, when I submitted the corrected manuscript to the printer, I felt strangely empty. I feel like that part of my life is over, and I wanted desperately to talk to someone else about it, but that opportunity was not available. I suppose it is now another transition period, and transitions tend to be uncomfortable. Yet You have already given me two other projects to work on, so You understand. Thank You for that as well. But I think I am finished with my first book. I don't know how long it will take to actually be marketed, but I think I have done all I am supposed to do.

Maggie, I do understand. Although there was never any deadline, you feel like one has been met. You want to declare "It is finished!" Yet there is no book to actually hold in your hand yet, so it is not quite finished. But it is no longer your job to get it done. And you don't even know how long a wait there is before anything else happens. But take heart, I have not gone anywhere, and all will be well.

Thank You, Lord for understanding. I feel a bit silly that I have all these strong feelings. But it helps to know You are with me and care about even such insignificant things. It was quite a journey to read the entire book in just a few days. I did not remember having been so close to You so many times. And the way You always encouraged me, and still do, how can I ever thank You?

You just did. And as you begin working on the next book, you will see and learn even more. You did not remember that I promised you that there were greater things ahead than you could imagine. Did you ever really think you would become an author? When you were struggling with having a consistent prayer life, did you think you could keep one for over two years without missing a day? Are you convinced that I am indeed leading and guiding you?

Yes, Lord, I am convinced. And totally grateful. And in awe of all you have been teaching me the past few days. The whole "conduit" thing has been going through my mind. I was thinking of how we are parts of the Body of Christ, and how our human bodies have so many conduit vessels within us. Miles of blood vessels, as well as other conduits all within each of us. It is mind-boggling.

Yes, it is, but now is not the time for a boggled mind.

Lord, am I avoiding working? Or just waiting for more inspiration? I feel like I am just spinning my wheels but should be getting somewhere. There are things to do, and they are getting done, but something is missing.

The frenzy, perhaps?

No, I don't think I would miss that.

It is several people who are no longer there to call or talk to. You are mourning at a time of what should be full of joy. It is a time to choose joyfulness despite your feelings. You are fighting pride over the published book. You are pleased with it, and delight in telling people about it, but are afraid that it is boasting. And loneliness is trying to creep in.

Then there are world affairs that are unfair and scary. So much that is not in your control. But I am still with you. I am

partnered with you in all your activities as well as your inactivity. I am guiding you, and loving you, and holding on to you. Be secure in My love.

Pain can be a teacher to you right now. You are acquainted with all sorts of pain. When you feel a headache, for example, you simply acknowledge that it is there, and continue with whatever you are doing. Either it will go away by itself, or not, but it does not stop you from functioning. It is the same with missing the people in your life that you would love to share things with. You realize it is painful and go on. If the pain continues or gets worse, you do something different.

Taking a Tylenol is like praying it through. You can talk to Me knowing I see both sides of life. Many times, you have asked me to give someone a hug on My side of eternity. I do not take those requests lightly. There is still a connection between you and those who are gone from this world. Love never fails. But the pain has to be transformed into fond memories. Rather than wishing you could talk to them now; be grateful for all the times you were able to talk to them over the years. Gratitude is your Tylenol.

Lord, that makes so much sense. Already I am feeling better about it all. I just wrote a book about gratitude, and You have to remind me to be grateful. I suppose that is an antidote to the pride, as well.

See, you are suddenly smiling again. So am I. It is good that you bring these things to Me. I love to help you sort them out. Rejoice in My love.

Thank You, Lord. I do rejoice.

The Lord had inspired me to pause and turn to Him during the small times of transition during the day.

Lord, I seem to have a lot of pain to offer You today. I also had a dream where I was given what seemed to be a simple task, but I could not do it well, because I could not read the directions. Yet, no one was upset with me that I did the job poorly. I received compassion instead. I remember being confused by that.

I did what You said I should do yesterday. I paused to praise and thank You at the small transitions of the day. It went well. It felt good that I kept remembering to do it. It was good to know I was obeying You.

This has a connection to your dream. When I asked you to come to me during the transitions of your day, you were not sure you could do it, but you were willing to try. The results were better in life than they were in the dream. Yet if they had not been, there would be no condemnation, just compassion. But rejoice that it went well. Do it again today but try to enjoy it a bit more.

It is good to obey – and this was not a distasteful task to obey, and you felt good doing it. Now concentrate on why I asked you to do it. It was an answer to your desire for union with Me. This is practicing union. Remember Brother Lawrence's book on practicing My Presence? This is doing that. In the past, you desperately wanted to do it, but could not. As in your dream, there was no condemnation, but compassion, for at that time you did not have the ability you now have.

You are surprised by compassion. You expect criticism or rebuke. I am not like that. In My love for you, I allow you to fail, only to help you to learn and eventually succeed.

Lord, I think You are telling me to use this in my teaching. I need to let my students try problems before they know exactly how to do them. Then show them how and learn how to avoid the mistakes that come so naturally. I tend to show them first, and not give them the opportunity to make mistakes. When You give me students again, I will try this.

Good. So how is your pain now?

It seems a bit better, but still there.

This is another lesson. When your mind is occupied with something else, the pain is not very important. This is why the pain seems more intense when you are trying to sleep. It is a matter of focus. Focus on Me and My goodness, gentleness, compassion, or anything other than your pain.

This is why I am continually wanting you to work on joy. Find the joys I put into your life and pause to fully keep your attention on goodness. That is why the passage in Philippians is so important. I need joyful friends and followers.

Lord, You are so right. We tend to get so negative, and You want us to become more positive – joyful.

Lord, one of the people I listen to on the computer said that we need to present our bodies as a living sacrifice and that means we have to give up all carnal sins. Does this mean I have to give up chocolate, ice cream, and eat foods I despise?

Not always. Moderation and politeness and listening to My direction must guide you. Your lack of sight, your lameness, and frequent exhaustion – without complaint – is a living sacrifice. Jesus did not self-inflict his pains and Passion but accepted it as His Sacrifice. Trust Me to guide you even in this – if I give you the gift of things you like, it is good for you to enjoy them. If, however you are served food that does not agree with your tastes and accept them – that is acceptable sacrifice. Keep things simple. Even sacrifice can be overdone and lead to pride and self-righteousness.

Thank You, Lord. He also said that once our bodies are under control, then our minds can be renewed.

Your mind is renewed every time you come to Me with your questions and concerns. It is renewed when you listen to Godly messages. I am doing all this. I am the One in charge of instructing you. Trust Me that I can do it better than if you undertake it yourself. Relax, chill out. Do what I ask: submit, surrender, intercede for others and your country and world and society. It will keep you busy enough.

I am not interested in you being miserable. Joy is much more effective in bringing others to Me. Keep working on joy and patience. Especially patience with yourself. If I would be displeased with you, I have ways to let you know. Otherwise, rejoice

in My pleasure and goodness and provision. Let My love for you occupy your mind instead of searching for things in your life that need to improve. I improve you. I know better what you need. Stop fishing for faults.

I get it! Thank You that You are in control. Please envelop me in Your Presence.

That I can and will do.

Lord, I will have much time alone the next few days. We are not sure what the weather will do, or if everything we are planning can actually happen. We will plan anyhow and leave the rest to You. In my times of solitude, I want to focus on You completely. I want to spend these days with You. Not because I have no other place to go, but because I just want to be able to spend more time with You. Don't let me get distracted.

Maggie, I will welcome the company. We shall have a party of our own. I have saints and angels ready to party. And My Father and Holy Spirit, being totally united to Me, will also be delighted. It will be a wonderful Christmas. I can help you plan. I don't often get to plan My own birthday party. We can have lights, and music, and I can even dance with you. And the Father will dance, too. It will be a couple of days of joy. We shall set aside all the troubles of the world and have our own party.

Lord, that sounds absolutely wonderful. Just thinking about it already has me full of joy.

That is what I want for you. Joy unspeakable.

Thank You, Lord.

Dear Jesus, Happy Birthday. Thank You for yesterday. I finished baking, and all the presents are under the tree. I turned on the Christmas lights, as well as prayer meeting music, and felt like I was, indeed, in Your Presence. We did not dance, but I did kind-of sway in my rolling chair while my cookies were baking. There were only three of us at Mass yesterday, but our priest did not seem to mind. I kept thinking that You said, "when two or three are gathered in Your Name, there You are in their midst." So, it was good. Today the Mass will be earlier than usual, but I am looking forward to receiving You once again.

And I am looking forward to receiving you as well. When you come to receive Me, I also receive you. I dwell in you, and you dwell in Me. It is what you pray every time, and I do answer such prayers. Delight in Me today, as I delight in you. I truly appreciate Your birthday present to Me in that you chose to spend the day with Me.

Lord, it is such a privilege to do so. Help me to keep this day holy.

How is the joy working out?
I can't tell any difference.

Keep listening. I will teach you. Remember that it is not just a feeling, but a choice. It, like love, is a part of the will. You need to choose it whether or not you feel it. Be aware of your thinking. When a negative or complaining thought comes, counter it with its opposite.

Lord, I need my focus back on You.

Yes, it is hard to keep a balance. There are many things to think about, and it is hard to keep it all in perspective. Do all the things as they need to be done. Use all the help that I provide. You have kept Me in focus through other activities. It all worked well. Take some time to rejoice. I am still here with you.

And Lord, I am so grateful. It is like I have a sanctuary each night when I can transition from what has happened to what needs to happen.

See, not all transitions are difficult. This was what you missed In previous service and ministry. A de-programming from the one day to the re-programming for the next. You wanted it to happen with other people but needed to learn to do it with Me instead. Now you see that I can and do provide such opportunities. And I can also cleanse you from whatever needs cleansing as well as strengthen you for what you will need in the day to come. All this happens when you come to Me daily. It is to be a joy to you as well as to Me. I love taking care of you. And I love that you enjoy taking care of others. Be at peace. All is well.

Thank You, Lord. It is so good to belong to You.

Maggie, just as there are times of trouble and pain, there are also times of blessing and joy. I have been telling you to focus on My love, joy, and peace. As you have done that, the feelings of love, joy, and peace have also emerged. You know you are not to be ruled by feelings, but when a positive one comes along, it is truly good. So many people are so bound up with the negatives, that they miss the blessings. Keep focusing on My gifts, graces, and blessings. They make the difficulties much easier to bear. You know the song well: "Rejoice always, pray constantly, give thanks in all circumstances, for this is the will of God in Christ Jesus for you." This is becoming a wonderful way of life for you. It is good.

Thank You so much, Lord.

Lord, I lift up all who are following You to the best of their ability and are attacked for their efforts. You gave us the example on the Cross, as You asked Your Father to forgive.

Now let me draw near to You and do what needs to be done.

Maggie be assured of My love and care. Do not allow the brokenness of others to steal your joy. I encountered opposition and hatred long before the Cross. But I did not allow that to affect My actions or attitudes. I did what the Father directed Me to do. There were times when it was more difficult than at others. But just as I had the support and comfort of My relationship with the Father and Holy Spirit, so do you. Keep doing each next good thing. Come to Me for help and support. I am always ready and able to give you what you need. Love and joy, especially My love, covers a multitude of sins. Do continue to pray and let Me handle the results.

Thank You, Lord. It is all Yours.

I have been practicing being thankful for whatever Your answer to my prayers will be. It really helped. I was much more aware of You through the day. Thank You.

You are most welcome. Keep it up today. A good habit takes a while to form.

Lord, my mind wandered off for a while.

I see. This is simply a temptation. When you feel My pleasure, the evil one comes to steal it away. But this time, you caught on. That is also good. My love and joy and peace are surrounding you. It is good to dwell in that. Do not allow being robbed. Know that your God is pleased. Spend this day enjoying that pleasure. As you do, you will see it multiplied. Not just your God's pleasure, but yours as well. I know your plans for the day are pretty mundane. Laundry, putting things away, perhaps a bit of cooking, but all these things can be done with a lightheartedness and joy as you feel the Father's pleasure.

I suppose this also requires practice.

Yes, and it will also require spiritual warfare. The enemy does not like seeing you happy. You will have many temptations to fight. Put on the armor you have. You will need it. Control of the mind is not easy. Banish all disturbing thoughts. When you find one encroaching, choose to return to My peace and joy and love. I will be right there to help you. And, yes, it will take practice.

It seems like it should be much easier than You describe it. But I know You are right. I do put on the armor and start with resting in Your arms until morning. Thank You that You give me such attractive challenges. I feel like I am in training, but at the same time, I feel like it couldn't be so pleasant.

Not all training is painful. When you are learning something, you really want to learn, the whole process of learning is pleasant. Especially when you see success easily. I have prepared you for a long time and you are ready for this now. In a fallen world, even happiness must be learned.

And learn I shall.

I see that no matter how much I have learned in the past, and how many times I have read or heard Your Word, there is still more to learn. We have now spent two weeks on Creation in Genesis and was amazed that You created the Sun on the fourth day rather than the first, so it would be obvious that it is a created thing, not a god as many peoples over the ages had thought.

It is true, there are many things to learn even when you have already learned much. I have given you a teachable heart so you can have the joy of learning continually. You felt this joy yesterday, and it was like an old friend. Welcome it back in your life as My gift to you. It is also your gift to Me when you see My ways with awe and wonder. We can rejoice together. In a world where the bad news is so often the main focus, it is important to see what produces joy and awe and wonder in your life. That is how your strength returns. Joy builds you up in a pure and holy way. Look for other sources of joy in your life. They are there. Seek them out. You will find them. And when you do, tell others of these joys. They also need to hear and rediscover them. You now have a new assignment.

Thank You, Lord. And that, too brings me joy. I love knowing what You want of me.

You provide all I need, so I don't worry.

Good. I don't want you to worry. Right now, it is a time of reaching out and reconnecting with people. It was good to speak to old friends.

Lord, I thank You. It is so good to be able to serve You through things that are also pleasant for me.

So many people think that serving Me must always be difficult, painful, or unpleasant. This is another lie of the enemy. I know and care about what makes you happy, and I use that in the good works I prepare for you to walk in. This is why I keep encouraging you to choose joy. Grumpy, unhappy people do not draw others to Me. You don't enjoy such people; neither do I. Do I love them? Of course, I do. But My desire is that they become happy, joyful people. I have come that you have life and have it more abundantly. An abundant life is full of joy and peace and love, and all such good things. Yes, there are difficulties and pain and all that, but I am with you through it all, and help you bear such things.

Yes, Lord, I have experienced Your tender touch especially when I had to experience much pain. Thank You. I am so glad I belong to You. You rescued me from so many things through the years and have given me a full and good life. I will never be able to thank You enough.

Your joy and gratitude bring Me joy as well. We can rejoice together. This is a wonderful part of union. Let's savor it.

Gladly.

A few days after revival started in Asbury, Kentucky, I was delighted.

The revival in Asbury is still going on, and it is very encouraging. A week-long prayer meeting, and Your Presence felt by so many young people. Please keep it going and spreading all across the country. Lord, You promised that You would heal our land. I believe this is the way You are doing that. I thank You and ask that You keep doing it. Show me how I can be a part of it all and help me do anything You desire. Lord, we have been hungry for a mighty move of God, and You are now satisfying our hunger and thirst for You. Fill us to overflowing and let us share the abundance.

Yes, I am doing a new thing. And yes, you do have a part to play in it. As you see and hear what I am doing in other places, do not forget what I am doing inside you. I can do great and wonderful things all around the world, and still be interested in the smallest details of your life. I listen to your global prayers, and also to your personal prayers. I am not too busy with worldwide affairs to pay attention to you. Omnipresence has privileges. I can hold you in My arms at the same time I can love and change and fill to overflowing the thousands and millions I am about to touch. I am delighted in your joy at what I am doing. I want you to keep doing what you have been doing. Relying on Me, getting closer to Me, bringing your days, plans, concerns to Me. The love, peace, joy and all the other fruits of the Spirit are not just for them but to continue to grow and produce more abundant fruit in you. There will still be struggles and battles and you are prepared to handle them with Me. Stay close to Me and hold on tight. There will still be bumps in the road, but I have strengthened you and taught you how to handle them. Let My joy continue to strengthen you. It is very good.

Thank You ever so much, Lord. I will stay so close to You that I cannot be peeled off of You.

Lord, You are doing some fantastic things. The prayer is still going in Kentucky, and other colleges are getting ignited as well. Please touch the Catholic Church too.

Do not worry, this is not limited to specific denominations. I will reach all who are willing to listen. Yes, I am doing something great, and I will continue to use you and all who seek My Kingdom. My love is for all. There are surprises yet to come. Keep praying and listening and watching. The lid is about to blow off of what I do. Be ready to pray with and for anyone at any time. I will bring people to you for a touch of kindness. And as you extend My love and kindness to others, you also will find it for your own situations. I cannot use you without blessing you at the same time. My love cannot flow through you without it touching you as well. I fill you to overflowing, and the overflow is for others, but you will be continually filled. No longer will you come to Me empty, needing to be washed or scrubbed. Your cleansing will be continuous as you stay close to Me. It will not take much effort to remember that I am with you. Union is happening. Rejoice!

Lord, I do feel it. And I do rejoice. When I first demanded union with You, I did not have any idea of what it meant, but I knew I wanted it. Now that I know a bit more, I no longer demand it, but gratefully welcome it. Keep me ever closer to You moment by moment. It is so good to belong to You.

I also belong to you. It is good.

As we prepared for a family birthday party, all my sons were coming to town.

It was good to talk to Karl on the phone last night, and they will stop by sometime today.

Lord, it is so great when I get to hug my sons. Thank You.

Just think of how great it will be for Me to hug all My family. There is a special joy in being able to do some things physically rather than spiritually. I do understand that. But the wait makes it even more enjoyable when it is finally possible. There is a resurrection of the body. And there is a good reason for it. But for now, enjoy all that you can and continue to do the next good

thing. I am with you and continue to sustain you. This is a time for rejoicing.

Thank You, Lord. I do indeed rejoice.

My oldest granddaughter is about to go to college. And my niece, Julie, only has four of the ten still at home. The kids are flying from the nest. I suppose that is as it should be.

It is. But I will never leave you. I continue to provide all you need. Keep following Me. I am leading you in new ways. It is good that you are not worried or afraid of it. This is progress. It is joy. Not the feeling, but the security. Joy combines with peace and love, and all the other fruits for your benefit as well as for those around you. I want fullness of joy for you. It is coming. Welcome it.

Thank You, Lord. You planted this seed in me long ago. I am so glad it has begun to take root.

Me too.

I am listening for whatever You want to say.

Maggie, My Maggie, hold on to Me. I am doing new and wonderful things for, with, and in you. I do not tell you ahead of time, as I want you to enjoy the discovery of all I do. The feelings and reality of My peace and love are to be enjoyed. And you give Me joy by your receiving them and your gratitude, as well as your contentment. Contentment is indeed a gift you give to Me. Yes, it is also a relief to you, but I had to work really hard to get you to this state.

And I truly thank You for all Your hard work. I would never have imagined that my happiness would give You joy. Yet it makes sense. I get joy from the happiness of those I love. Why wouldn't You? You are revealing Yourself to me even in this. Thank You.

Yes, I am. But it is not just a surface happiness I look for in you, like a child getting a toy he wanted, but a deep knowledge and appreciation for being loved and cared for. This is the contentment that is so delightful to Me.

I did not have any idea that my reaction to things could affect You. I suppose I have been so self-centered that I only considered how I felt, not how You might feel.

And how others also feel when you react in certain ways. When you show joy, it enhances the joy of others. Work on that.

I will. And I thank You.

Lord, I am listening. What is on Your mind?

There is a whole universe out there on My mind. But that is not what we need to talk about. Contentment is good. Joy is beyond that. You have been noticing some instances of joy. It also contains awe and wonder. Sunrises and sunsets, a happy baby, My Presence, have all touched you with joy. Keep looking for it. The more instances you find, the more they will begin to counteract the current culture of negativity. When joy is constant within you, there is no room for fear, or any other negative emotions. I want My joy to be fully rooted in you. Then there will be abundant good fruit.

So, producing fruit is not only "doing" things?

Exactly. Remember the mother of one of your friends? You only saw her once. Yet you tasted her good fruit. All you saw in her was that in her old age and severe disability, she was joyful and kind, and a pleasure to be around. You decided right then that you needed to practice those things while you were still young, so that when you are old, you can also be like that. She never did anything to teach you or help you in any way, but just her disposition taught you much. Her light was shining. Yours must also shine. Joy is a beacon of that light.

Lord, I have just found another source of joy. Learning what You are teaching me. I am full of awe and wonder. Thank You.

It also gives Me joy that you understand. Enjoy this day. Think on these things.

I will.

Lord, the lesson yesterday about joy truly touched my heart. But I did not follow through during the day. Perhaps today I can meditate on it a bit more, and find more sources of joy in my life.

Just thinking about it is not what is needed. Practicing is. Seek and you shall find. Also, find the difference between pleasure and joy. Then see what are the ways joy can be stolen from you. When your expectations were totally sidelined, you experienced a loss of joy. You can guard against that. It is a part of not just submitting and surrendering, but finding the joy and the trust to see My hand in things as they proceed.

Lord, now You are continuing to teach me. Thank You. I was feeling distant from You for some time. Yet now, I feel the closeness I have been missing.

That is a lesson for another day. Right now, keep your focus on joy. There are opportunities waiting for you to discover how much joy I actually put in your day. Yes, I put these things in there. You usually go through the day without even considering that I am involved in the day. Trust, submission, surrender, supplication have been just concepts that occasionally are needed in your life. But when you see Me behind every moment of your life, they become constant companions. They have the power to crowd out all the negatives that afflict you.

I think I am feeling the awe and wonder or joy at what You are telling me. Thank You.

Now go about your day and practice this. It is a learning process that needs lots of practice.

Keep reminding me through the day.

I can handle that.

Chapter 4

My Peace I Give Unto You

I was able to watch a 3-hour program last night and rededicated myself to Your service. I am sure that My relationship with You is solid and growing, but felt it was good to give You all that I am and all that I have once again. Lord, I know You are perfecting me according to Your plans and timeline. Help me to cooperate with You rather than try to tell You how and what to do. I know I love being taught by You.

Maggie, I accept your re-dedication. I also appreciate that you are not trying to take back the control of your life and training. I can do it. Really, I can, and will. I am kinder and gentler than you would be, and thus you are not as likely to rebel.

Lord, I feel Your peace. Thank You.

Rest in this peace. No more teaching for now. Just rest in My arms. You do make your God smile.

Thank You, Lord.

Lord, I have no concerns to talk about right now. Do You?

How about you enjoying a bit of peace?

That sounds really good. But what can I do or say now?

Just enjoy.

Lord, your peace just swept over me. It is wonderful. Thank You.

It is My gift to you, and always available. Learn to avail yourself of it more often. I do not withhold it from you, but you are not used to seeking it. And you have an enemy that wants to steal it from you. It is coupled with My Love, and Joy. You need all three. There are several trinities in My Kingdom. The main one is Father, Son, and Holy Spirit. In your childhood, you used to start many assignments in school with JMJ, Jesus, Mary, and Joseph. The three theological virtues of Faith, Hope, and Charity are also a group of three. As are Love, Joy, and Peace. You like the number three because you were born on the third of the month. I like it as well. See, here is another way there is union. You were made in the image and likeness of God. Though this is such a small likeness, it is something to enjoy having in common.

It is so great to think of having such things in common with You. Lord, thank You for such a gentle and kind time of prayer this morning. I have been so concerned with world affairs and with the illnesses of my friends, that I forgot to enjoy all Your ways and gifts. Today, I feel such sweetness and kindness from You. I see how much I need that. Help me to pass it along to others as well.

That is exactly what I desire for you to do. Set all the heavy issues in the world and in your life at My feet. I can handle them. Let the kindness and sweetness sink into every cell of your body and soul. It is cleansing and refreshing. Now you also feel My hand upon your head. My love is washing over you. Savor it. Be still and know that I am God. Not the god others think I am, but the One Who loves you with an everlasting love and cares for your every need. Go rest in My arms. Let me handle all that would upset you. I want you to fully experience My Love, Joy, and Peace.

Thank You so much, Lord.

In _Grace and Gratitude_, I spoke of being God's pitcher. It is when the Lord uses us in the life of someone, we are like a milk pitcher, full of *something that is good and nourishing. But when used up, we can sour if not washed.*

Lord, I received a phone call from a very troubled person. I wanted to assure her of Your peace, but I don't think I was able to help her.

Would you like a better way to handle the pain others struggle with?

I sure would.

While they are speaking, begin to pray in the Spirit silently. When possible, find a humorous story to change the subject. All along, listen to My leading. I will help. Then after the conversation is over, come to Me for cleansing. I will have used you as My pitcher. Yes, she is hurting. But she cannot see any solutions. You cannot offer her any at this time. But giving her a different topic to think about may be helpful. Start collecting such topics in your mind. Animal stories are a good start. Eventually, you can insert a bit of wisdom, but don't try to solve her problems. You cannot. But steering the conversation to more positive things may help. Availability is more important than ability. The ministry of presence is important. Keep bringing her to Me in the Spirit. I know how to reach her. But it may take some time.

Thank You, Lord. I also bring others with problems to You. They need their eyes opened as well.

I know. I am also working there. Be at peace. I can handle things that you cannot.

In the middle of my prayer time one night, I stopped to finish a task I had started earlier.

I just remembered that I tried refrigerating my roll dough yesterday, and I just made what I hope will turn into hamburger rolls. I was afraid to leave them until morning as they were rising in the refrigerator. I need not do such things without considering the timing.

Making bread while you pray is not such a bad thing.

Thank You for understanding.

Believe it or not, even making bread can be My Will for you. So many things you do that are just second nature to you are indeed My inspirations. You are just beginning to see how very involved I am in your life. So often you think you are forgetting Me, yet I am directing your every step.

It's that invisibility thing again.

It has its advantages as well as its drawbacks. One of the advantages is that I can work without scaring everyone. Another is that I can be with you at all times at the same time I am with others around you. If I were visible, it would be so confusing. Remember when you did not want My second coming to come? You were afraid that if I were there in the flesh, you would be somewhere in the back of the crowd and could hardly get a glimpse of Me. While now, you can converse with Me at any time. The thought that I am everywhere only works with invisibility in the physical world. In the spiritual world, it is not as confusing.

Does that mean that heaven is not physical, but only spiritual?

Not exactly. The word "only" makes you think it is less real or important than the physical. The vastness of the spiritual is beyond your imagination. It is to be discovered only in the next life. It is not wrong to wonder about it, but the total understanding will come later.

I have enough trouble figuring out this side of eternity, so I don't usually think of the next life.

That is perfectly acceptable. Right now, your job is to live in this world while beginning to grasp the spiritual as well. The peace I give you helps you accept even what you do not completely understand. I do give you glimpses of what is to come, so you don't get discouraged when everything does not go well. There is much good yet to come. You also need not worry about not being able to communicate with Me even if I come in the flesh soon. I will make provisions for all you need.

I sort-of understand that now. Can't completely imagine it but am content to believe You. Let's concentrate on the current situations. The rolls will be done in a few minutes, and then I need some more sleep.

I can handle that.

And the world situations that seem to be so horrible?

I am working on those as well.

Right now, I have nothing to worry about?

Did I not tell you that worry is useless? I want you at peace and full of joy. All the other things are My job. Trust Me. I do My job well, even if many in the world think otherwise. There is much good yet to come. Concentrate on the good.

I will draw near to You and rely on Your Holy Spirit to guide me. Just as I need to choose each night to come to You, and now I have the attitude, for which I thank You, that I refuse to be robbed of my time with You. I must have the same attitude so I will not be robbed of doing something You asked me to do. Sounds good in theory, doesn't it?

I will indeed help you in the practice. See, you have learned a lot. You are beginning to see that your feelings are often evidences of an attack of the enemy. In a world that values feeling more than truth, no wonder so much is in a mess. But I am working on it. Keep praying and listening. I may be working behind the scenes, but I am working.

Thank You, Lord. Somehow Your peace is upon me. And I am so grateful.

Good.

Lord, today I want to rest in You. Let me spend the day focusing on You. As I had said, I am very grateful for belonging to You.

And I am delighted that you do. Today, at least for part of the day, I will have you to Myself. It is not like the times on a retreat, but it can be just as good here. Come to Me and let's just

enjoy each other's company. I will give you My peace, and you will give Me some peace and joy as well.

Lord, I never thought of You wanting peace before.

Relationship is not one-way. When you experience peace and joy, I do as well.

Wow! Thank You Lord. You have been teaching me about how we are made in Your image and likeness, and that seems to fit.

Near Christmas, things at my house usually get hectic, but the Lord wanted me to focus on His peace.

I did not make any progress with the decorating, but perhaps today. It was, however, a delight to be helpful to one of my grandnephews.

Maggie, this is what I was telling you about to let My peace guide you as to the activities leading up to Christmas. There were things you wanted to get done, but instead, you took the time to help your grandnephew learn something he wanted to do. You were ministering to Me. And you enjoyed it as well. I will provide all you need. Yes, even the time. Right now, My peace is upon you. Let it do what I send it for.

Thank You, Lord. It is great to be able to do things for You.

Dear Jesus, thank You that the house is presentable. I will need much help. I will have more time tomorrow for whatever You set before me.

Lord, the news is still pretty distressing, but we will still keep waiting and watching for what You are about to do. I hope we can put some new materials I ordered to good use.

But for the next few days, family will be in the forefront. Please help everything work out well.

Maggie, it is all connected. God, family, and country. You are turning to your God for guidance and direction. You are cooking

and planning visits with family members. You are concerned for your country and plan to study to see what you can do to better affect the society. All simple steps, but My hand is upon you, and it is good. Even small annoyances can be handled, and there is no panic. I am with you. The peace you feel right now is My gift to you. Keep coming to Me with your plans and projects. Your book will soon take shape. The struggle is a part of the process.

Thank You, Lord. I do want to be constantly at Your service.

We were planning a prayer meeting while only one or two could attend:

We will obviously need all Your help. Please be with us, whoever "us" happens to be. I think I will make cookies, just in case anyone comes.

Maggie, do you see what I see? There is no worry or panic in your prayers. You are bringing Me whatever concerns you, but you have a peace about it all. I assure you that I can handle all your concerns.

Thank You, Lord. But what can I do for You? You are blessing me in so many ways.

Right now, your gratitude and peace and joy are My delight. It is also good that you are more aware of the Father's love. And praying in the Spirit more is also good. But be alert. Do not let your enemy steal from you. Keep close to Me, and I will keep you at peace. This is a time of blessing for you. Savor it. Remember it when times of temptation and trials try to crowd into your life. I am with you in peace as well as in trial. Lean on Me.

Lord, I am savoring Your Presence and gentle peace. I don't think I can write any more. I am just basking in Your love.

It is good. Keep doing that as long as you can.

Lord, it is your birthday. Let me spend today and tomorrow much more aware of Your Presence. I still have much to do, but I want to do it all with and for You.

So, you want to combine Mary and Martha today?

Yes, I suppose I do. You have a way to make me smile. I needed that.

I know. Despite all your efforts to stay calm and at peace, the desire that everything be done well is creating its own stress. But I am with you, and all will go well. Do not lament the traditions that are missing this year but be grateful for the more peaceful celebration. It is good.

Thank You, Lord. Hold me close.

Lord, I'm not sure who or what I am at this stage in my life. All I know or want is to totally belong to You and be whatever You desire. Teacher, mother, grandmother, nun, caregiver, wife, are all roles I have had, and learned from. But even though I still get to use some of the skills I learned in those roles, they do not take up most of my time. Now there is author added to the list, and perhaps once again, student. But totally Yours, a child of God, I suppose that is the most constant and important role I have. Thank You for it.

Changes in role are inevitable. You have had quite a few of them over the years. I experienced a few Myself. But looking at them as gifts, rather than calamities, is very good. And you are correct that in all these changes, the one constant is My love and care for you. You are Mine. I am yours. Every day you give Me yourself, and every day I give Myself to you. I do not take your offering yourself to Me lightly. You do not take receiving Me lightly. It is good to keep learning and to be willing to try new things. But the greatest importance is the belonging you are so fond of. You do belong to Me. And thus, you belong wherever I put you. Whether it is in the solitude of your house, or in a group of people, I have a purpose for having you there. Love is who I am, and who I want you to be. It is what makes you happy, and

what pleases your God as well. It can be expressed in so many ways and will motivate you to do things you never imagined you would or could do. Keep at it. It is good.

Thank You, Lord. I thought I was confused, but now I am encouraged. And Your peace has also enveloped me. I don't think I can ever thank You enough.

Thank You that the fire of Your love has grown in me, but please let it be blazing.

That has always been My plan. It is why I put a desire within you for total union with Me. You have recently heard some things that resonated with you. "It is hard to love someone if you don't know them." You are getting to know Me and your love is growing. Remember on your wedding day after the ceremony, you felt you had made a commitment to be with Rae the rest of your lives, and yet you felt like you hardly knew him. But as time went on, you felt like your love for him was like a parachute opening, and what had been small and compact, billowed out into something huge and beautiful. Sort-of like the mustard seed. There is beautiful growth as well as intricacies that are yet to be discovered. There are nests in the tree and all sorts of adventures to be had.

Not to mention all the adventures we have already had. Lord, I do thank You for knowing me and loving me. Don't let Your grip on me loosen up. Hold me tighter and tighter until I am so much a part of You that I cannot be peeled off.

That, too, is My plan. Be at peace.

Lord, I don't even know what we can talk about now. Holy Spirit, I seem to need Your help......

Lord, You have given me peace, but the world is gearing up for war. Even our spiritual leaders are at odds with each other. Our Church needs courageous leaders, our country needs a total overhaul of its leaders, and You seem to be waiting for more of us to turn to You for help and direction. It is hard to understand it all.

I have not called you to understand everything, but to trust Me, submit to Me, surrender to Me, and to pray (supplication). The understanding will come later. I give you peace, love, care, and all you need. You give me the trust and the three s's. Notice that I do not call you to trust others, or submit or surrender to others, just to your Triune God. Listening to others is good but be cautious not to take them too seriously. Do the next loving thing when you are not sure what to do next. Or do the next practical thing if there is no-one around to love. Like you just started the dishwasher when you could not think of how to pray. Simple mundane things do need to get done. But do not worry. I have given you peace, and I want you to stay at peace. A bit of joy would be good, too.

OK, Lord, You managed to make me smile again. Thank You.

I enjoy your smiles. You see, I need some enjoyment, too. I see all the troubles you have spoken of as well as a whole lot more. But My joy comes from the relationship with those who are near like you. That you come to Me even when you don't know what to talk about. We managed, didn't we?

Thank You, so much, Lord. Hold me close.

Lord, I feel like You are holding me in Your loving arms. Your peace has come upon me again. Thank You.

It is the comfort of obedience. You are willing to listen and do what I have been telling you. Trust, submission, and surrender are meant to be peaceable and pleasant. Most people do not understand that. But it has to be trusting Me, submitting to Me, and surrendering to Me. I am the only One that can give you the peace that results. And the third S is also important. Supplication is appropriate. Do not be afraid to ask. I often wait to act until My people ask, not because I do not want to give them what they want, but because I want them involved in what I do. It is in this

way that You can do the "even greater things" that I spoke of. It is not that you can do them alone, but that I do them through you. Remember that I said that I only do what I see the Father doing? It has to be the same with you. To do the greater things, you need to be so connected with Me that you ask for what I want done and let Me do them through you. It is you doing them, but I am the hand within you, the glove.

Lord, I want to be so connected to You that You can do these things within me. Open my ears, my eyes, and my heart that I can know what You want done. We all need You so much. I am so thankful that I feel like I already have You. Belonging to You is the answer to my need of You.

Now how do you feel?

Even better. Your peace is so strong, and I thank You.

I am at Your service, listening and delighted to belong to You.

I am also delighted that you belong to Me. You are becoming more aware of Me during the day. Taking a nap in the afternoon was also a good idea. And you are more aware of your needing My help and not as self-sufficient. At this time in your life, that is a good thing. When you were younger, it was good for you to have some independence. You had to learn that there were many things you could do if you were willing to try and persevere. But as you get older, you also learn that you cannot control many things and need to rely on Me and others for much more than you would like. This is a normal cycle of life on earth. You come in helpless as a baby, and you leave helpless in old age. Yet there is much learning all along the way, and when you are aware of My participation in your life, there is much joy and peace as well. Keep on learning to depend on Me. Just as you were delighted with each new skill your children learned when they were babies, I am delighted with each new way you now depend on Me rather than yourself. In youth, the learning is to do things, in old age, the learning is to let go of things. Both can be difficult, but both

can be lovely with My guidance and participation. My grace is sufficient in all cases.

Lord, thank You that even the frustrations seem to be manageable. So many things that used to be important to me, are now just situations that will eventually be handled. Like the sink leaking – I am glad it is fixed, but a few years ago, it would have been impossible for me to wait several weeks before it was done. I also don't know when my kitchen floor will be repaired but I can wait without worry.

Yes, it is the worry that causes so much trouble. I want you free from worry. When you are in charge, many things can worry you. When you let Me be in charge, I take that burden off of you. Fear and worry are both toxic. That is why I keep telling you to avoid them. Rest in My arms again. Let My peace envelop you.

When there was a revival at a college in Kentucky, we were preparing for a prayer meeting at my house:

Lord, please come and let us join with what You are doing in Asbury. Come with Your power and peace and touch each one of us.

I am coming. In fact, I am already here. You feel My peace.

I do, indeed. Lord, when Your peace comes upon me, I can't seem to have anything to say. It is as if I have no cares in the world, and just feel happy and content. Is this normal? Is that what they are feeling in Asbury and why they don't want to leave the prayer meeting?

I can have that effect on people. I deal with each one according to their need. Some need repentance and forgiveness, some need to know My love, or joy, or peace. Many need to know I am real. I meet each one as they are coming to Me. And it is so good that they are coming. Rejoice with Me. I love working this way, where I am not as invisible as I have been for some time. You are not the only one frustrated with My invisibility. But right now, many will be able to see what I do. It is very good. And I am delighted in the love and joy that you and others are experiencing and returning to Me. Worship is also union. It is not difficult,

but natural response to knowing Me as I am. **When you feel My peace, you enter into worship. That is why you need not say anything, but simply enjoy the union you have so fervently sought for many years. Right now, it comes in short segments. As you get used to it, it will stay longer. It is meant to be enjoyed. Both by you and Me.**

Lord, there are no words to thank You enough. Perhaps silence is the only way I can respond.

Lord, I seem to be scared by this Lent. I am trying to leave the control of my life in Your hands but seem so uncertain about everything. I feel weak both physically and spiritually.

It is in your weakness that I can show Myself strong. And you know you can trust Me to do so. Yesterday you relied on Me, and it went well. Today, you know you have to rely on Me as well. Take it one day at a time. There is nothing you have to do alone. I am with you always.

Thank You, Lord. I just want to curl up in Your arms and have You hold on to me. My body hurts in many places, and walking has been difficult. Even coming to the kitchen this morning was a struggle. But You are right. When I am weak, You can show Yourself strong. If You don't mind, I will go back to bed and rest in Your arms.

Yes, and feel My peace come over you as well.

Thank You, Lord.

Dear Jesus, thank You for all You did yesterday. By morning, most of my pain was gone, and it was not a struggle to move.

I also had my first failure as to Lenten eating. I did fine until during my class I decided I wanted some of the cashews I have in the freezer. It would have been fine if I had just had a few, but once I started, I did not stop until I knew I had overdone it. Thank You that it did not affect my sleep. Help me to avoid such temptations today.

Consider being forgiven. But it was not just a lack of moderation, but a pride that it was not sweets. Pride comes before a fall.

Guilty as charged. I think I was trying to impress You. And it did not work well. Help me to listen to You rather than my own desires.

How is that being scared that bothered you last night?

It seems to have gone away. I suppose I was afraid of failing in Lenten disciplines. Now that I have already failed, it does not seem as scary.

You see, I can even use your faults to bless you.

Is this an example of "all things work together for good?"

It is. And how is the pain level now?

Quite low. Thank You.

You see, a little humility is not as painful as you expected. This is also a small example of "where sin abounds, grace abounds even more."

Yes, I do see it. I am grateful for Your forgiveness as well as all that grace.

Now go back to sleep in peace. And I will enfold you with My love.

Lord, I am confused. I don't know whether I am to be grateful or ask for healing about my emotions. I seem to not have any. Or at least no strong ones. Is this a gift, or is it something You desire to heal within me? Or am I fishing for defects? A few days ago, I realized that one of the reasons I felt like I was feeling like a spectator of my own life was that I had stopped wanting to learn. The courses I am taking sparked some life into me, and I was grateful. Now I am aware that it seems like my emotions have been "capped" like a well that is no longer in use.

Do you trust Me?

I think I do.

Then leave this question in My hands. If that well needs to be re-dug, leave that to Me.

I think I can do that.

Just focus on whatever is before you. Do the next good thing. Do not allow fear and worry to attack you. Bring all your cares to Me. I can handle emotions as well as the lack of them. Contentment is not a deficiency.

Thank You, Lord. Unless You tell me otherwise, I will treat it as a gift.

I seem to be lacking energy this morning, so I will need to rely on You. That sounds terrible. I need to rely on You whether I have energy or not. I am just more aware of it right now.

Yes, but when you are aware of your need, that is when I can work best in your life.

I see. I seem to be more emptied of myself. Sometimes I feel like I'm ready to do Your Will, but now I feel more like I'm ready for You to do whatever You Will. I suppose it is not a bad place to be.

I agree. I want you to be receptive of My love and peace and joy. Today it is not more knowledge you need, no exercise of your brain, but a deep experience of My Spirit.

That song is still reverberating within me. "Holy Spirit, You are welcome here. Come flood this space and fill the atmosphere..."

The space I want to flood is your soul.

Is there anything I need to do for You to do that?

No, just receive. It is like a car being stopped at a gas pump. It does not do anything; something is being done to it. You simply need a re-fill. I can do it here, or you can go back to bed, and I can do it while you feel My arms around you. You already feel My peace. Go and let Me continue to revive you.

Thank You, Lord. I receive.

Dear Jesus, this morning I do have something to bring before You. I have had pretty vivid dreams, and I am grateful for them. But in my dreams, I am never quite sure of myself. I seem to know what I am doing, and what I need to do, but things are not usually working out the way they should. I have a lot of frenzy as I often did when I was young. Both in my dreams and in reality, I am still fighting battles, but am I fighting the wrong battles? I'm not sure this makes any sense at all, but I woke up tired, and the day is just beginning.

It does make sense to Me. You are indeed fighting battles. Some seem to be going well enough, but others are not. Your tendency is to try to fight by yourself. It wears you out. It is once again a matter of who is in control. When you are in control, everything depends on you, and it is more than you are equipped for. When you look to Me for each step of the battle, it all depends on Me, and things go better. You need a big dose of peace. My peace. Not an artificial peace that masks what is going on underneath, but deep abiding peace. It means everything is in My hands, and you go through the day with Me. Follow Me. Do not try to run ahead or lag behind. Hold My hand and stay right alongside of Me. You will have things to do, but not alone. Do only what I have you do. See how this works today.

Thank You, Lord. I needed that.

Lord Jesus, thank You for all You are doing. both in my life and in the world. Somehow, my contentment is lacking again. Our conversations are getting shorter and shorter, and I always seem to be exhausted. You are gracious and kind in sending me back to. bed, and still giving me strength to get through the day, but I once again feel undisciplined and distant from You. I am so sorry about my complaining. It seems I am never satisfied.

It is good that you are not satisfied. Last night you prayed for more of My Spirit in your life. Wanting more of your God is a good thing.

Lord, many years ago I listened to a message that contrasted monastic and apostolic lifestyles. The monastic was well-ordered with definite times for most everything.; usually governed by the times of prayer. The apostolic, was governed more by the mission while fitting prayer in wherever possible. It seemed to me that it does not just apply to religious life. Some people are more comfortable with specific times for everything. Their lives have to have a constant, relatively unchangeable schedule. Others are much more flexible and do things according to what is needed at the time, regardless of schedules. It seems I have admired the monastic style but am wired for the apostolic instead. It is not that one is better than the other, just that they are different.

What do you want to do about it?

That is what I do not know. My grand and glorious plans usually do not work. I need Your plan.

I do have a plan, but you will have to wait a while for it. You do better when I reveal My ways to you in small increments. That encourages you to rely on Me and stay closer to Me. Right now, all I will tell you is to watch, listen, and pray. I am not telling you when to do it. See how that works. But be assured that I am not discontented with you. I am delighted that you want more. Let My peace overtake the discontent.

Thank You, Lord. It is working. I think I can sleep a bit more now. Please wrap Your arms around me and hold me tight.

I can certainly do that.

Dear Jesus, thank You for all Your help yesterday with a job You gave me. It took several hours, but somehow You focused my mind so completely on it. Then I still had time to do some studying, and now that is also finished. Thank You. Usually, Saturdays are hard to fill up, but yesterday was great. Thank You.

How is the discontent?

It seems to have been replaced by gratitude.

As it should be. Do you know why?

I think so. Is it because I asked You for a change rather than trying to change things myself?

Yes. And I did not tell you the whole plan, but you were willing to leave it to Me. Your entire day was flowing without you directing it.

I did not even notice that when I came up with difficulties, I did not ponder how to get through them, but they were solved. Was that You, Holy Spirit?

It was. And you were not frustrated by the difficulties, or the time it took to solve

It did not even occur to me that You were so closely helping me. Thank You. Even the phone was not incessantly ringing. I was able to completely focus on the job at hand.

The night before, you asked for a refreshing of the Spirit baptism. How do you like that answer to prayer?

So much so that I ask again. I will need Your help much today. It is Mother's Day, and there are no plans with my sons or grandchildren. Other than possible phone calls, I am not expecting any other celebration.

It is similar to your birthday, but that turned out well. Trust Me to make the day special. After all, your motherhood was a divine gift.

That it was. And I certainly thank You for it.

And you are certainly welcome. Now rejoice in this peace. Rest some more, and embrace the day knowing I am with you, within you, surrounding you, loving you.

I could never thank You enough. Your Presence is delightfully overwhelming me.

It is good.

Dear Jesus, thank You for calling me this morning. You were right, it is so much better when I answer Your call than when I determine that I must come at a particular time. This way it is an act of love, the other way it is out of duty. Thank You for showing me this. I simply have a better attitude when I come because I feel You are calling me. Even the thought of You calling me makes me feel loved and appreciated. Yet, duty is not a bad motive, either, but it seems like the difference between a servant and a friend. I love being Your servant, but being Your friend is such an honor!

And I am delighted to honor you. You honor Me with your care and friendship not just for Me, but for many others. Remember My one commandment. Love one another as I have loved you. I have no commandment that you must be a perfect housekeeper. Neither do I require a particular weight you must be. I don't require many things people expect me to. But your love, freely given, either to Me or your brothers and sisters, that is most precious to Me. That is one of the reasons you have the opportunities I give you to be kind and thoughtful toward others. You appreciate the chance to touch others, they appreciate your kindness and care, and I watch with delight. And in this case when I say "I," I am referring to the entire Trinity. It warms My Father's heart to see His children's kindness to each other. It warms the Spirit's heart to see that His teaching and guiding are bringing forth good fruit. And I, the Son, am honored that you are imitating Me.

Lord, I am speechless. And glad to be so. I feel Your pleasure. You gave me such an opportunity last night. I knew it was Your gift to me both to receive kind words, and to be able to listen for a long time to stories I had already heard. But You gave me this gift of being able to listen and be kind to elderly folks. As I am also getting up in age, I am grateful that I have others around me with that gift as well. And You, Who are always willing to listen to me, I really appreciate You. In fact, Your invisibility is not even bothering me right now. The person I was talking to last night on the phone, I could not see her, either. But I could hear her, and with us humans, at least one of those sense is necessary. But You have taught me to "hear" You in a different way, and it is so good to be able to converse with You this way.

Are you happier with our communication today?

Absolutely. Thank You so much. I have felt like I was only waving to You when I came for prayer lately. Today I know we have connected and spent some quality time together.

It is good, but also shows that you cannot be controlled by feelings. We do spend quality time together at various other times throughout every day, but as they have become the extra-ordinary efforts and prayers and kindnesses you provide. Just as you are grateful for ordinary gifts I give you, as well as the special ones. It is very good. Now go and rest. You still have four hours you can sleep peacefully in My arms.

Thank You ever so much.

As to my spiritual issues, I really don't know how things are going.

That is why I keep telling you not to "grade" such things. Let Me handle it all. As you go through changes, things will seem chaotic. But it is usually only when looking back over a period of time that you will see progress. I see it all, beginning, transition, and end. If I see a problem, I am fully capable of letting you know. And I will also give you all the grace you need to correct things if necessary. Peace does not mean that there are no struggles. My peace is in the fact that I am the One in charge and taking all the responsibility for your progress. You follow Me. Let Me take care of everything else.

Lord, how is it that I feel like I am again in the beginning after all these years?

You know the song: "The steadfast love of the Lord never ceases. His mercies never come to an end; they are new every morning...." Every new thing has to have a beginning. It always feels like you are just starting out. But all the new beginnings build upon each other. No progress of the past is lost. It just has to be less important in order to work in the present new beginning. Keep trusting Me. I am a master teacher.

That You are. And I am ever so grateful to be Your student.

Things are going well, and the contentment is back. Thank You.

You call it contentment; I call it peace. It is not exactly the same. Contentment has the focus on you. It seems to be generated by you. It is as if you had control over it. Of course, you know that it comes and goes, and you have very little control. But peace is a gift you receive. It is My gift to you. Notice that you are or are not content, but you have peace.

I see it now. Thank You for Your gift of peace. I suppose happiness also fits in there somewhere. We are or are not happy. But it is Your gifts that make us so.

Close but not quite right. Happiness is also affected by your perception and assumptions. Some people have gifts others would love to have, yet they are unhappy because they are blinded by many other things. But let's keep peace in mind. You feel peace that overcomes you. It feels like it comes from outside of you. It needs to work its way to within. The deep abiding peace I want you to have is indeed My gift, but it has to work into your innermost being. It is My Holy Spirit. Still a gift, but no longer outside but within. This is why peace is a fruit of the Holy Spirit. It has to grow within you. I plant it there, but you have to nurture it. You feed it with prayer and trust. You water it with everyday good works. Soon it produces fruit you can share with others. But it is still My gift to you. Because with each of the fruits, the Giver comes with the gift. As you accept and rejoice in the gift, it is like delighting in the Giver, and letting Him delight in your joy. It is union. It is very good.

Thank You so much, Lord. It is indeed very good.

Lord, thank You for the teaching on peace vs. contentment. I felt your peace all day yesterday, and I was content, too. The day went really well.

Yes, they are to work together. It is not that the two are opposed to each other, just that they are different. Both are necessary. Today, continue in My peace and look for joy as well.

How does joy strengthen you? You sing "the joy of the Lord is my strength." Is it? And how can it become true? Think on these things.

I will. A good project for a Sunday.

Do you notice that your peace is slipping away?

Yes.

Do not allow that. Keep relying on Me to guide you. Do not second-guess everything you have done thus far. Keep listening and trusting Me to sort it out. If you make mistakes, learn from them, and go on. Remember that we are partners in all endeavors.

Lord, thank You. I just want to hold on to You and have You hug me so tight that I am completely embedded in You.

What can stop you?

Absolutely nothing.

You need a Fatherly hug. The Father is delighted. Enjoy His embrace. Sink into the ocean of love and know it is endless.

I am in awe. Thank You so much.

Stay there as long as you need to. And know that it is a place you can return to any time.

Lord, it seems I am more engaged in my life now. Sometimes I feel like I am simply watching my life go by, but right now, I am OK. Thank You. I am not worried about anything, knowing You are in charge and will take care of everything. But I also care about these things, in a much healthier way.

It is because you are engaged in an activity that seems to have more purpose. It is healthy. It has a definite goal and needs to be done as quickly as possible, but not frantically. It is good.

Lord, it is so good that You understand us.

And it is also good that you are bringing all these things to Me, rather than worrying about them. My peace is having a good

effect on you. Hold on to it. Hold on to Me. I am with you. It is good.

Once again, words are not enough to thank You.

Come, Holy Spirit, and show me how to pray right now. How can I best worship my God.

Right now, just enjoy My peace and Presence. You asked, and here I am.

Lord, I feel like I am on the mount of Transfiguration. It is good for me to be here. I do not see You, but I know I am in Your Presence. And it is all I need.

No questions?

Not right now. Just enjoying.

Me, too.

Lord, right now, I think I am in a holding pattern, waiting for the next assignment. And I never know if it is something You are doing or if it is some deficiency on my part. Am I waiting on You, or are You waiting for me to process something I should have understood before?

Restless?

I suppose so.

Is it so hard to understand that I can give you rest?

It shouldn't be, but I miss the times of You teaching me great and wonderful truths. My prayer times have shortened to just a few minutes.

But how much of the rest of your day and night is devoted to Me? It used to be that Your prayer time was almost the only time you spent in My Presence. Now you listen to teachings and study and spend other times with Me. Don't worry. I can get your attention in many ways. Let My peace take hold. This is a time I am working within you. It is not for instructing others through your

writing. **Consider it as being at a spa. You are the one receiving treatment, not the one giving it. Relax and enjoy.**

Thank You, Lord. That helps.

Lord, I thank You that You are ever so close to me. It is so good to belong to You. It is indeed good.

You are now living in My peace. Yes, you still have occasional times of turmoil, but before, you lived in turmoil, with occasional times of peace. Trusting Me has been a difficult lesson for you. But I am pleased with the results. As you should be as well. Now enjoy the peace and rest some more. I will guide you through this snowy day.

Thank You, Lord. Yes, I am pleased. And along with Your peace comes that joy that has also been hard for me to learn. Thank You.

Dear Jesus, thank You for a clean house and a good night's sleep. It is Ash Wednesday, as well as Valentine's Day. I am not sure I am doing all the praying we are expected to do, but I will check on that this afternoon. But You have been with me, and I thank You. I have been given Scriptures to consider:

> John 14:27; Peace I leave with you, My peace I give to you. Not as the world gives do I give it to you. Do not let your hearts be troubled or afraid.

> Proverbs 3:5; Trust in the Lord with all your heart, on your own intelligence do not rely.

> Psalm 51:12; A clean heart create in me, God, renew within me a steadfast spirit.

Peace, trust, and a clean heart. Lord, one word stood out that I had not noticed before. You said that You "leave" Your peace with us.

I just remembered that You 'give' Your peace, but now I see that it is not a momentary gift, but something that lasts and is available any time. And with that peace, we have the ability to calm our troubled hearts or fear. We are not to 'let our hearts be troubled or afraid. You give the peace and leave it so we can control our fears and troubles. Then trusting in You, rather than our own intelligence. Once we have Your peace abide with us, trusting You is much more natural. Intelligence seems to speak to me more than "understanding.' I always considered myself intelligent, though there are many things I don't understand. But even intelligence is not to be trusted, as there are many intelligent people who are very troubled or afraid.

The third quote, from PS. 51, has been the cry of my heart. Create in me a clean heart. Lord, I want to be totally clean before You. But it seems like it is simply a wish, and no matter how much I confess or repent, I do not 'feel' clean. But it is You who have to create that clean heart within me. It is not my own doing. You renew a steadfast spirit within me. I believe You.

It is true. I am working in many ways in your life. You have felt My peace many times, but now you need to remember that it does not dissipate but is available any time. Your trust is growing. I did give you your intelligence, but you have seen that it does not meet all your needs. I do. As for the cleansing, it is an ongoing process. Your house was cleaned yesterday but will need to be cleaned again. It is the same with your heart. Do not let it be troubled over this. Just as My peace is always available, so is My forgiveness. And it is My love that cleanses you. That is also always there. I am always there. Rejoice!

If I can just remember these things, it will be a good Lent.

Chapter 5

Patience, His and Ours

Lord, is there anything for today that You want me to be aware of?

It will be a busy day. Stay open for My guidance. You will find Me as you seek Me. I am delighted that you are seeking Me. Are you aware that I also have been seeking you? Yes, I do know where you are at all times, but the union you seek is also what I seek. Neither you nor I will be satisfied until it is accomplished – yes, this side of eternity.

Lord, that is so encouraging. Thank You.

You are welcome. It is time for encouragement. There have been so many discouraging things both in the world and in your life recently. But the tide is turning. Keep looking for encouragement. I AM still in charge – both in your private life and in the world. FEAR NOT!

Please show me what my part is in what You are doing.

Right now, your patience and continued intercessions are needed. I do see your struggles in this, but do not give up. I do listen to your prayers and use them in this time of war. Consider your prayers as ammunition for the armies of heaven. Much needed. You have volunteered to fight beside Me. This is a part you have right now.

There will come a time when I will ask other things of you, but for now, know that your prayers and love are needed and helpful. Stay positive! Do not doubt that victory is coming. I am with you always. Even things that seem unimportant to you

are precious to Me. Energize one another. I have given you great companions – stay in touch as much as possible. I am with you.

Lord Jesus, I don't have much to do today.

Maggie, I can keep you busy if you want.

Yes, Lord, I do want that. I want to serve You more actively again. Is that possible?

With Me, anything is possible. Wait and see.

There is that waiting again. You are not only teaching me joy, but patience as well.

I'm glad you noticed. Both are needed. In your retirement, you tend to forget them.

But I do a lot of waiting.

Yes, but now you need to add the virtue of patience. Just because you have to wait a lot does not make you patient. Just like a smile on your face does not necessarily make you joyful.

So, I'm missing something. I really need to look up the definitions of both joy and patience.

See, you already have an assignment.

I accept the assignment. I'll let You know what I learn. It is good to be learning again. I did not even notice that I was no longer interested in learning anything these days. I was just glad I still knew the math I was teaching.

Writing again opened up several things.

My life was getting boring, but now I seem to have come back to life. Thank You.

You are welcome.

Maggie even if it takes a long time for you to learn some things, do not doubt that I am teaching you. I rejoice in this relationship and you can do so as well.

Come Hoy Spirit, show me how I can better serve my God.

Right now, your waiting and listening is an acceptable sacrifice. There are times I simply want your attention. Even when I do not seem to speak great truths, just being together is good. You like it when I teach you. At those times it is your mind that is active. But you are more than just a mind. You offer me your whole self: body, soul, and heart.

Heart is not the physical muscle in your chest, but the spirit within you that is capable of relationships. It is where the affections reside. It is where discernment dwells. It is where I reside. The Kingdom of God is within you because the King resides within you. When you invite the King to come in and give yourself to His service, His Kingdom is within you. All three Persons of the Trinity come. There is no separation in the Trinity.

This time of personal prayer is your opportunity to commune with your God and King. It can be time of conversation, but it can also be simply being together. In any friendship, conversation is important. But there are also times of doing things together.

The intimacy grows in many different ways. Knowing each other's likes and dislikes, sometimes thinking along the same lines, caring for each other, encouraging each other, knowing each other's past and present, being able to read each other's feelings—all are part of intimacy.

You can and do have such intimacy with friends. That is why I call you friends, not just servants. But to have such intimacy with your God, can be overwhelming and difficult to believe possible. Yet, that is what you desired and signed up for. It is what your God has desired and created you for. It is growing inside you. It is meant to completely take over your life.

But it does not happen instantaneously. It has taken many years to get you to come to Me regularly. You have yearned for total union with Me long before you had any idea of what that means. Yet you still wanted it. Now you understand much more, but there is still much more you have not yet comprehended. I put that desire in your heart – because it is also My desire. As you rely on Me for everything, you will see it happening. Rejoice in the process. It is good.

Lord, I am grateful for all You are doing with me and for me. I am trying to be content but see how far I still am from relying on You for everything. Listening for Your voice constantly seems so difficult. Yet I desire it. And I believe You put that desire within me. So, You must have plans to fulfill that desire.

Yes, you are right in both those thoughts. I do want you to hear My voice at all times. And I do plan to fulfill it. Be patient with yourself as well as with Me.

Lord, both a smile and Your Presence came upon me. You asking me to be patient with You seems backwards. But You are right. I have been impatient with You. I'm sorry.

Apology accepted.

Lord, I thought I was a pretty good teacher, yet You are teaching me how to still become better. Thank You. I used to think I was pretty patient, too. But You are still teaching me patience.

And as long as you allow Me to do so, and cooperate with Me, you will continue to grow in virtue and see good results. It is good that you see that even when I am teaching you something, I am on your side. If young people understood this about those in authority over them, they would have a much easier life. The fallen nature struggles against authority even when it is for the benefit of a person. If you can teach this to your students, it will benefit them greatly.

With Your help, I will try.

Lord, I ask now that You come and be powerfully present to us as we meet for our prayer meeting. We need You to revive us, so we can be Your instruments in this revival that we are so yearning for.

I am with you now and will certainly be here when two or three gather in My name. I know how difficult it is to wait for what you know is going to happen. Whether it is a good thing like a revival, or a difficult thing like My passion, the waiting is difficult. But after it happens, it was worth the wait.

Remember how difficult it was to wait when you were getting ready for surgery? You knew it would be painful, but that was not why you were anxious to get it going. You were anticipating the eventual result of less pain. This revival is like that. You know some things will be painful as the necessary cleansing must take place, but you are looking forward to a better life with many more people following Me.

You listen to the news waiting for both the removal of the wicked, and the turning of many to Me. Yet you only see a little at a time. I did not see many turn to Me while I was on the earth, either. Especially not from Pilate's palace. But much of the world changed in due time. The key is to do what I did. Keep in touch with My Father and rely on Him. Though I wished that the fire was already blazing, He kept Me calm and willing to wait until the proper time.

No matter what was ahead of Me, I desired His Will. Unite your will to Mine. As this union grows, even the waiting is redeemed and will be time well used. Now go and rest a bit more, and let My arms enfold you.

Thank You, Lord.

Lord, there was a powerful message we heard yesterday. It confirmed a vision from our little prayer meeting. We seem to be on the same path as those we listen to. Thank You. Help us to pray alongside them and be a part of what You are doing in our world.

It is good for you to see that I have you positioned just right in this battle. You need to see that your little group, small as it is, is a part of something much greater. There is a uniting of My people despite what has been a much-divided Church. Focus on the union that is possible. Set aside all differences and come together in purpose and prayer.

Rejoice in the technology that makes all this possible. Yet, it has been used for a lot of evil, but it is also being used for much good. I am working on many issues. Be very patient. I have placed the right people and angels in various areas and given them their assignments. Yours is to continue to listen, intercede, and stay close to Me. Keep working on being positive.

Let praise and thanksgiving flow from your mouth. Encourage all you meet that I am working regardless of what is perceived by the world. Find the silver linings in the dark clouds that are covering the earth. Point them out to each other as well as those I send your way.

Do not give in to fear. I am providing all you need. Just as you are not alone in this, neither am I. Yes, I have the power to do what needs to be done, but I choose to use you and many others to help and take part, an important part, in the process. There is a great awakening coming. I have awakened you sooner than many others so you can be partners with Me in bringing in a great harvest.

Lord, we are at your service. Thank You that You are empowering us who are old, blind, lame, often hurting, yet happy to be useful to You. It is such a privilege to be partners with You.

Now, Lord, I am listening and hope to hear Your voice.

Yes, here I am. It is good to get together with family. Enjoy your time together. I will be right with you, invisible as usual, but definitely present. See, I made you smile.

That You did. Thank You. I seem to be needing to lighten up.

I know. There is much happening at this time of the year. But I have assured you that it will all be fine. Just take one step at a time, and do not worry about anything. It will all come together well. I am in full partnership with you in all you do.

Lord, I am so privileged to be in partnership with You. Let me be a good partner. Let me look to You for direction, and don't let me lose awareness of You.

Aware of Me or not, I am here. Be patient with yourself. I do not leave you when you are absorbed in the events of the day. I am delighted that you are fully engaged in what you do. Your life is to be lived. I also live in you. It works whether you are thinking about it or not. Be secure in My arms and enjoy your company. I will also enjoy it all.

Thank You, Lord. Let me rest in Your arms.

Lord, thank You that Your peace is again coming over me.

Yes, it is My gift to you. And your receiving it is your gift to Me. Remember when you were so frustrated in the chapel, years ago, when you could not seem to pray? You did not understand that I was giving you peace. Now you can see that just pausing and feeling My gifts can be a wonderful time of union with Me. It took 75 years to calm you down enough so you can receive this gift. Yes, I see that smile.

Remind me of that when I get frustrated with how patient You are.

I can do that. When you are looking for My justice, you get frustrated by My patience with others. I do not desire that any should perish. Not even the ones in the news that seem to be causing so much harm. But when you see how patient I have been with you; you are beginning to see why I delay the justice others deserve. This is why I kept telling the people to "judge not."

How often do you judge Your God? I know you do not do it outright, but many times you wish I would do things differently than the way I do them. Trust Me. I do know what I am doing.

Are you not glad that I did not repay Saul for persecuting My people, but revealed Myself to him instead and I am still teaching multitudes through Paul's writings? I have many Sauls I am working on right now.

You did not think you would be writing books on prayer, when over the age of 75, either. My ways are sometimes surprising. But it is My love that you need to see behind every event. Look for and find My love. You will also find peace and joy and all the other fruits. Let Me surround you with My love.

Lord, You are amazing. Thank You.

Dear Jesus, thank You for Your amazing grace and forgiveness. Once again You proved that being convicted of sin by You is such a loving and empowering encounter. Along with the conviction, You provide the power to overcome the sin. Thank You.

Maggie, it is good. You are now aware of My great love for you as well as for those you encounter. You see that My love is not dependent on your performance, intellect, or any other aspect of your being that the world considers important. I can be pleased or saddened by what you do or experience, but My love for you is total and complete and will never change.

It is not something easy for people to comprehend. Unconditional love is unexpected by the fallen nature. Many need to be convinced that it even exists. That is why I need My people to be ambassadors of My love. Your job is to tell others that I love them. It is the job of My Holy Spirit to straighten out their lives. You were taught this long ago. It bears repeating.

Lord, help me to do my job well, and not to try to do Yours. There is a peace in knowing what our job is, and also knowing we are capable of doing it well. You have had to teach us so many things. Thank You for Your infinite patience.

It has taken many years, but I had been praying my special prayer for a long time, and finally began to see the results:

Maggie's Prayer:

> Lord, let me or make me and help me:
> Trust You completely,
> Be obedient to You in all things,
> Be wise in Your ways,
> Be a pleasure in Your sight,
> Be a credit to Your name,
> Walk with You, talk with You, and abide in Your love,
> Be continually filled with Your Holy Spirit,
> Do the things You do and want me to do,
> Know You, love You, and serve You more each day,
> Live with You eternally.
> Lord, You are doing marvelous things. Thank You.

I do a lot that cannot be seen. This is why I keep asking you to trust Me. Your prayer starts with trust. It is good. I have been answering that prayer. You are trusting Me more. You are more obedient. You are growing in wisdom. You are a pleasure in My sight and a credit to My Name. And union with Me is growing. You are beginning to know me as I am.

My love is changing you for the better. You are finally relating to Me more as a friend than as a servant. I do appreciate your service, and you have not stopped serving Me. But loving friendship is so much better. Belonging means a lot to you. It does to Me as well. But it is a reciprocal belonging. Not ownership, but family. Not servitude, but love. On the outside, these things can look the same. But at the heart level, they are vastly different. It is good to know the difference.

Lord, it also takes time to learn the difference. Thank You for taking so many years to teach it to me.

Dear Jesus, thank You for Your patience with me. I have had several opportunities to come to You, but kept putting it off, as the bed was warm and comfortable. You assured me that whether I got up to come to You or not, Your love for me would not change. But I could not make You wait any longer, so here I am. And You seem to be playing with time again, as it is not even 4 AM when I was sure it would be closer to 6 AM. Perhaps it is not time that You are playing with, but my perception of time. Either way, I thank You.

I seem to be reluctant to work at writing during the day. I have great ideas at night but am not putting them down. Is this just an attack?

It is. The enemy wants you to doubt your abilities and motives. You are also desiring something I have not provided, while ignoring Whom I have provided.

True, Lord. I have been wishing for human direction not only in regard to writing, but everyday life as well. Yet You have given Me Your Holy Spirit to guide me in all my ways, and rather than allowing Him to direct me, I secretly seek the unavailable human to spur me on to do what I know I should be doing. How do You manage to put up with me?

Aren't you glad that I love you? Love covers such things. But love also does not leave you there. Today, rely on My guidance through Holy Spirit. The song "Holy Spirit, You are welcome here" has been reverberating in your mind for several days. Make it true. Recognize the reluctance as the attack of the enemy. Resist it and choose to do each task you are avoiding. And when done, rejoice in My arms. I do provide all you need, including times of rest.

Lord, how do You do it? You convict me of what I would consider something horrible, yet You leave me feeling completely loved and understood and valued.

It is what I do, and Who I am. Stay here in My Presence a while. You feel My hand upon you and need not say or do anything. Just a silent hug. Then go back to sleep until morning. It is all good.

I may not completely or even slightly understand the Trinity, but I do feel that I have been Fathered, redeemed, and guided. Many times in the past, I have asked to be enclosed in the embrace of the Three Divine Persons, and that is what I have been feeling now. Thank You.

As Lent is coming to an end, I need more direction for my prayer times. I have been conscious of the season but have avoided contemplating Your Passion or death. You know I always have trouble with that.

I also had trouble with that. But as you are battling with physical issues, and others around you are also battling with their own issues, you are living out and uniting with My Passion. I accepted it patiently, and you are accepting your own share of it patiently.

Suffering is a fact. But so is new life. There is a reason Lent comes around the end of winter and beginning of spring. You cannot just immerse yourself in the pain and suffering, you need to see the flowers bloom, the weather getting warmer, and birds singing.

There must be a balance. Do not neglect either side. It was My love for you that helped Me endure all the suffering. I neither resented nor fought it. I gratefully accepted any help along the way. When Abraham was asked to make his sacrifice, He also did it without resenting or fighting it. But his willingness was enough at that time, and Isaac was returned to him.

I had to go a step farther, and actually give My life, but it was also returned to Me three days later. You and those around you who are facing difficulties, need to know and follow in the same way. Do not resent what you must endure, but accept any help along the way, and trust that there will be a good return. I am with you through it all. And you are with Me through it as well.

Today I think I will need a nap, as sleep has been difficult. The leg cramps have been severe.

When you have these pains, don't forget to patiently unite them to My pains. Mine were caused by the cruelty of others, yours are caused by other factors, but they are pains, nonetheless. They can be an occasion for union with Me. And when they are gone, then you can rejoice with Me. I do not want you in pain. But some pain is inevitable. It is not to be feared, just endured. But uniting it with Mine, it can have redemptive value. Now try to rest a bit more. I will strengthen you.

Dear Jesus, I don't even know how to approach you as I am in disobedience. I am again living Romans 7. The good that I want to do I am not doing. I want to repent, but I can't seem to actually do it. It is not that I don't know how, You have taught me well. And You have not withdrawn Your love or care for me, but my reluctance to come to You is a sure sign that I am wrong. As is my inability to let You speak to me for more than a few minutes.

The fight within yourself is fierce. But I have given you the means to win. Come to Me later in the day.

Dear Jesus, thank You for not letting me get too far from You. You touched me during the Holy hour. So, I resolved that I would stop running away from You and do what You have been asking me to do. I only worked for about a half-hour, and finished what I could, and the rest of the day went much better.

Lord, I am here to thank You for Your forgiveness. And Your patience as well. At least I am not hobbling in disobedience.

Maggie, it is good to work together again. Your reluctance to tackle My directions was because you forgot that I am doing it with you. You were overwhelmed by the amount of work it will take, and felt you had to do it alone. That is a lie. Believing lies always causes trouble. It is not the amount of time you spend in obedience that matters, but that you are ready, willing, and able to do so. I have never asked you to do anything beyond your

capabilities. And I also accompany you when you are doing anything I ask of you. I will give clear instructions.

Thank You, Lord. I think this will be a great help. Now please wrap Your arms around me once again as I try to sleep a bit more.

I will be delighted to do that.

Lord, the world is getting more and more upsetting, but I'm sure You are aware of it. There are glimmers of hope here and there, but overall, we are in such trouble that only You can straighten it all out. Please do so soon.

As for me, though, Lord, You have been wonderful in Your love and care. I do thank You.

Do not worry about the world. I have said that in the world you will have trouble, but I have overcome the world. Keep watching and praying. Not worrying does not mean not caring. Your part is to pray, and to follow My leading in conversations with others. My part is to lead many others like you as well, until the necessary changes will come. Do not let discouragement take hold. The changes are coming. I will take care of you through them all.

Thank You, Lord. I do trust in You.

Dear Jesus, thank You that You are indeed working in the world. I do pray that people would once again become lovers of truth. Lord, You are the Way, the Truth, and the Life. Please reveal Yourself to the nation.

I am doing just that, but it takes some time for people to awaken. It is happening. Much of it is below the surface still. But truth will win out.

Filling up empty spaces in your day is difficult for someone who prefers being with people rather than solitude. You are not yet at a place where My invisible company satisfies you. It is where you are heading, but not yet there. Be patient with yourself. I am. You need to look for ways to enjoy those empty spaces. I purposely am not filling your life with too much activity. I am drawing you close to Me, even when you think you are failing.

Lord, I thank You for understanding and continuing to teach me.

Chapter 6

Kindness

One night after deep intercession I closed my notebook and turned out the lights, the Lord kept teaching me. He brought to my mind the Scripture where the self-righteous said to Him, "Lord, Lord, did we not prophesy in Your name? etc." and He replied "Away with you. I never knew you." But this did not apply to those who did not or could not turn to Him. He put us in their lives so we can introduce them to Him by praying for them. Then when they come to His kingdom, He can say, "I know you did not know me, but I knew you because one of My servants told me of you. And their prayers have brought you here."

I don't know if this is theologically correct or valid, but I believe the Lord, in His kindness works this way.

What is on your mind this morning?
Not much, I think my mind is blank.
I can work with that.
I'm glad. I think You have to pick a topic to talk about, as I think a large part of me is still asleep.
But you are here. Would it surprise you that I appreciate your putting a priority on having this time of prayer? How would you feel if one of your loved ones went against their comfort just to spend time with you?
I would feel very honored.

As do I. People are very easily aware of offending Me. But do not realize how much honoring Me actually affects Me. I gave you feelings because I also have them. You are made in My image and likeness. I feel and appreciate love and honor and affection as much as you do. Even more. Being infinite, even feelings become infinite.

I have been teaching you about the positive aspects of life. I also look at the positive much more than the negative. You have found ways to please Me. Can you even imagine infinite pleasure? You can easily picture infinite displeasure, and expect lightning to strike, or the hurricane that is now raging. But even though people quote that God is love, they seldom associate positive feelings with Me.

I am not only wanting you to be loving and kind, but I am also loving and kind. I do expect you to be thankful, I am also thankful. I have all the good qualities you enjoy in friends and family. I am family. Yes, you belong to Me, but I also belong to you. Not to be taken for granted, but to cherish and delight in. I cherish and delight in you. I spend time with you just as you spend time with Me. Your love gives Me comfort and pleasure. Your kindness to others gives Me satisfaction.

All the virtues you desire to have in your life, I have in infinite ways. That is why I tell you to learn from Me. Trusting Me should not be a difficult task. Imagine infinite goodness. Imagine pure pleasure. No hint of the negative in My pleasure.

When you think of pleasure, there is always a part that makes you think there is something wrong in it. When you eat something you really like, you think you should not. That is the fallen nature that keeps you from completely enjoying things. I can enjoy your love and kindness without that hint of negativity. I do not fear losing your love while I am experiencing it.

Remember how your aunt would be upset when her son visited her, because all she could think of was how lonely she would be when he left? I do not do that. When I walked the earth, I did not live in fear. Fear robs you of so much. I want you free to live in the present. Many people miss the joys I put in their path because they are focused on something they fear. I want you to be fearless. Be aware but fear not.

Lord, thank You.

Lord, as my house guest is leaving today, she feels like she has learned a lot through this visit. She is also delighted to listen to the teachings I so enjoy. Lord, is this evangelization, one person at a time?

Yes, and no. What she has learned will have a ripple effect on people you do not even know or could reach on your own. Your book is also working in the same way. As you care for just one soul, you do not see all the others that will yet be affected. You do not know how many others you have affected in the past, either. Just as you have recently heard about good deeds you did in the past and were surprised that the memory of them is still cherished by others, so there are many that have been touched by Me through you.

Even your patience with the elderly is helping others. You need not do great and heroic things all the time to serve Me. Even little, insignificant kindnesses become something wonderful. It also need not be difficult or unpleasant. I can work with what has become a joy and a pleasure in your life, to serve and be kind to others. My Will is not always something to dread. I work through your natural talents and gifts. I gave them to you. It is also My joy to see them accomplish the purpose for which I sent them. This visit has done you as much good as it did for Pattie.

And, Lord, I cannot thank You enough. You have shown me how wrong my (and our society's) attitude toward You has been. I don't yet know how to teach others all You have shown me, but I certainly want to do so.

Right now, you still need a balance. In the past, you have experienced much pain and sorrow, and are still experiencing some of that. But now you are much more aware of My love and kindness and gentleness. You know about My power and strength

and justice and mercy and have a hard time sorting some of that out. You long to see the spectacular but are learning things that seem quite ordinary. But be patient with Me. Much of what I did and taught My disciples was quite ordinary, and yet are still taught through Scripture today.

Thank You, Lord, for ordinary things. They can be extraordinarily wonderful.

There are a few of us who try to have a prayer meeting a couple of times a month. Sometimes as many as six of us come, but sometimes people's lives and health prevent them from coming. This particular time, only one person came.

Lord, my friend and I had a lovely time talking, but we did not actually have a prayer meeting. I now feel we should have at least asked You to come and join us, but we so enjoyed each other's companionship, that somehow, we did not focus much on You I am so sorry.

Do you think I was not there? How many times do you have family or friends come to your house and have great conversation and you simply listen without saying anything? Do you not enjoy having them there even though you are not a part of the conversation? You are happy that they came, and you were interested in their lives and stories they told. Were you ever offended that you did not seem to be the center of attention? Of course not. You were happy they were there and enjoying themselves. You did gather in My name. And I was right there with you. I am not as easily offended as you thought I would be.

I guess the Act of Contrition I have learned as a young child makes it sound like You are easily offended. It starts out, "O my God, I am heartily sorry for having offended Thee." We get such distorted views of You from the strangest places.

I know. This is why you need a relationship with Me, rather than relying on what you learned or thought from what others taught you. Misconceptions come so easily. It takes long and hard

work to correct them. I have been working long and hard to get you to see Me differently than you used to.

And I am so grateful that You have. But I think I am still missing the balance. I see that the "fear of the Lord" is not really fear, but awe and wonder. Yet I do not want to fall into presumption and think everything I do is OK. There is still sin, and I know I am a sinner. But lately Your kindness and graciousness have so overwhelmed me.

Lord, thank You so much for such great friends and family.

You were worried that all the favor I have shown you would go to your head. Yes, I have been gracious and gentle and kind and understanding. But pain still comes, and your disabilities have not disappeared. This is part of the balance you were looking for. Even if you are aware of My kindness and Presence, there are parts of your life that cannot be ignored that are not so pleasant. You are not to focus on these things but bear them knowing that they are simply part of the fallen world and temporary. I do provide relief, and you have experienced My favor.

Remember Paul's thorn in the flesh? It was so he would not be so elated that he would lose all track of reality. When your heart is burning within you, it is easy to forget that all is not perfect. You do need to pray and fight and endure. But My kindness is always available to give you rest and a taste of what is yet to come.

In the past, it was much more difficult for you to focus on the good when confronted with pain and loss. I was always there with My love and care, but now you see it more clearly. It is good.

Lord, now I can see how we can be grateful even for pain. You use it to teach us, and we usually miss the lesson.

That is why My patience has to be infinite.

Once again, You made me smile. Thank You for both Your teaching and Your patience. It is so good to belong to You.

Lord Jesus, thank You that in Your kindness You take care of all my problems.

I can handle these problems. Be at peace about them. Be at peace about how I use you. Yesterday was a day of service. Today, you need refilling.

Lord, do I need a washing, too?

It is already done. Many times, in the evening and during the night You turned to Me and I took care of that. Your awareness of Me is increasing. My love cleanses you, and you have been immersed in My love.

Is it sort-of like taking a swim vs. a shower?

Yes, both wash you. But swimming is not just perfunctory. It can have more of a fun and pleasant aspect to it. Not something you "should" do, but one you can enjoy doing. The refill is the same. I do not require special acts of piety; I simply want you to enjoy My company. Like going out to dinner. I am inviting you out.

I gladly accept Your invitation.

Good. Let us enjoy this coming day.

Whenever I get discouraged, The Lord always brings me back gently.

Lord, I feel like I am getting distant from You again. I know You have not moved, so the problem must be on my side.

It is discontent once again. Two days of relative solitude.

Of course, You are right, but other than repentance, how can this be fixed?

Different media.

You mean instead of the TV; I should listen to music or watch one of my DVD's?

Try that. But don't be reluctant to pause occasionally and move around and speak to Me.

I do feel like I have been neglecting You while wishing I had someone to talk to.

It is a learning process. Some people yearn for more solitude, others, like you, would rather have less. The trick is to enjoy both and be able to transition easily from one to another. Once in a while you may have a balance naturally, but not always. Gratitude is helpful. Do not be afraid of talking to Me when there is no-one else around. It is not the same as talking to yourself. If there is no-one there, then no-one will think You are crazy.

I will try. And I will let You know how it goes. I expect it will be uncomfortable for a while.

I comfort the afflicted and afflict the comfortable.

I knew that about You. Thank You for the smile.

Now do you still feel distant.

No, Lord, it seems to have vanished. Thank You.

After a short visit to the hospital, I became very aware of other people's pain and hurts.

Help us to learn what You taught about other people's problems. That we are meant to understand what hurts Your heart about their situation, and that we are to do what we can that is good and kind. That we are not to let their problems hurt our hearts, but simply bring them to Your heart.

It is similar to not taking up other people's offenses. When you hear of an injustice that another suffered, it is not kindness to get angry at the offender. You do not have the grace to forgive that person. The offended one does. You can listen, advise, and pray, but you cannot afford to harbor ill feelings against the offender.

In the same way, when someone you care about is having difficulty, your job is to help and console and pray, but you are not to take on their emotions. Your job is to bring all the problems to Me, as I can do what you cannot. It is a matter of focus. You focus on My love and care both for whoever has the problem and for you as well. Let your prayers for others lead you into thanksgiving rather than the pain they are feeling.

Compassion is good but should not be carried for long. It is as if the person who is hurting has a heavy package to carry. You want to help them carry it, but you cannot take it all on yourself. You can, however, through your listening, and prayers, help them put the package on a wagon which will make it easier for them to take it wherever it needs to go. I am the wagon. Once you help them get the package onto Me, you do not have the package to carry, and they can manage to take it from there with My help. The burden is then on Me, and not on you. They will still have to take it where they need to, but you have been kind and helped them lighten their load. But you cannot break off a piece of their burden to carry it yourself.

Lord, yesterday, I was weak, and had trouble carrying a bag. A friend offered to carry it upstairs for me and put it in the car. Then the bag traveled with us and neither of us had to carry it, as it rode in the car. She no longer had to even think about it. She went home, and we went on with the bag in the car. Hours later, when I got home, I was able to carry the bag into the house myself. You were the car. You carried it most of the way and allowed me to regain my strength to carry the bag again when I needed to. By this time, my friend had probably forgotten about my bag, and so she should have.

Thank You, Lord for this teaching. It really helps.

Maggie, I am with you. I am doing a new thing even within you. After spending over two hours worshiping the other night, it was good. But now, you are not sure of how to approach Me outside of the formal praying that you do.

Thank You, Lord, for understanding. I feel like I am back at the beginning of learning to pray. As if I don't even know how to begin.

That is why you have the Holy Spirit.

Come, Holy Spirit, I seem to need instruction.

You have already entered the courts with thanksgiving, so now come through the gates with praise.

I see, I need to get my mind off of me and the things around me, and begin to think of Who You are, all three Persons.

Father, I come to You first. You have loved me and provided all I need. You are Creator, all knowing, all powerful, all present, and all loving. In Your gentle care, I have been nurtured and fathered. You gave me faith to get to know You and You sent Jesus to allow me to become His bride. Lord Jesus, You came not only into the world, but into my life. You hold me each night and strengthen me during the day. You allow me to feel Your Presence and love and You give me Your peace. Holy Spirit, You work so quietly in my life that I often don't even realize You are guiding and helping me. Yet You continue whether I am aware or not.

See, it is good. And it is enough for now. You can sing unto Me, and bless My name. In the morning, look up Psalm 100 again.

Lord, Your kindness and gentleness are so comforting. Thank You.

Lord, it has been a while since we had deep conversation. I am asking You. What can we talk about?

If I do not have much to say, it is not necessarily a problem. My love does not depend on how much we talk. Neither does your love. You did pray, I was not absent from your life. Your typing prayer sessions may not be as long as they have been, but neither am I neglecting you, nor are you neglecting Me. Be at peace. I have ways to get your attention when there is something important to discuss. But I appreciate your coming to Me daily to see if I have special information to give you. I especially like that you enjoy having My arms wrapped around you when you go back to bed. I also enjoy that. This is a time of blessing for you.

I remember a homily on how we are a Eucharistic people. Just as You took the bread, blessed it, broke it, and gave it. You also have times when You take us, that is accept us or give us a sense of belonging. At other times You bless us, as You say this is a time of blessing.

Then there are times when You break us, the difficult times of suffering or cleansing. And then You give us to others as we have a bigger or better message to give them. I thank You for this time of blessing and Your kindness.

See, the Holy Spirit is working by reminding you of things you have learned before. This, too, is communication with your God. As you have heard, remembering is re-living the graces and blessings of past times, and the power that comes with it. I am with you. Enjoy the company.

Lord, I want so much to be everything You want me to be. Though You are not complaining, but always so kind and encouraging, I still feel I have so far to go. Hopefully I have finally learned that only You can make any progress happen. All my striving is counterproductive.

I am glad you have learned that. It is perfectly good to just rest in My arms, and wait for My instructions. There is a peace in that. When your dog was younger, you had to be careful about opening the front door, for she would often rush right out and run around the neighborhood and cause you much grief. Now that she is older, she still loves to go out for a walk if someone will take her, but she no longer tries to escape her boundaries.

You are like that as well. You see that I provide for all your needs, and can be secure in allowing Me to decide what needs to be done next. You do not desire to reach out and handle everything on your own. And I don't have to go and find you and bring you back to where you belong. Yes, you do belong. Just as your dog now knows she belongs to you; you now know you belong to Me.

And I am so delighted to belong to You. Thank You for all the training it took to get me this far.

Lord, You are indeed doing something new in me. I know it is Your kindness at work, and I don't have to understand it, but just cooperate. I think that is what I am doing.

You are cooperating. You are learning to rely on Me much more. I am guiding you in shorter, but more frequent spurts. It is My plan. Yes, I still have a plan for your life.

And I am happy that it is enfolding. You asked for total union with Me. It is in process.

I remember saying "I will not be satisfied until I have total union with You". I think I am now very close to being satisfied. Thank You.

But I, on the other hand, will not stop with satisfaction. I came that you have life and have it abundantly. There is more than just satisfaction. Wait and see.

I will indeed wait. And I continue to thank You.

Lord, there is not much on my mind today, how about Yours?

It is the usual, Keeping the universe going, Big issues, little issues, but always interesting because I deal with people. I find people very interesting. Don't you?

Actually, I do. That is why teaching never bored me. Even if I taught the same lesson five times a day, the students received it differently, and communicating it to them made it interesting.

Here is another aspect of being created in the image of God. There is much difference between God and man, but there are so many similarities, too. Look for the similarities. It will encourage you. The differences are also worth looking at and should inspire awe and wonder.

It is the same with any relationship. There are always similarities as well as differences. Learning to appreciate both, makes life wonderful and unifying. Divisions are caused by wrong interpretations of both. Union is not eliminating the differences but appreciating them. In the current society, people need to re-learn kindness. Thinking the best of others, including the differences. Treating people with dignity. Many have lost that.

But it can be taught and re-learned. Let's work together to accomplish that.

Lord, I am delighted to work with You.

Chapter 7

Goodness and Generosity

Lord, I forgot to take my slippers off like I usually do when I come to pray. I figured that if You told Moses to do that, I should also.

I appreciate acts of reverence, but I am more interested in the relationship than the form. There is nothing wrong with proper form. But it is not enough – there must be power, and the relationship is the power. When I went off to pray, sometimes all night, I was in relationship with My Father. That is how I knew His Will and received the power I displayed.

Holy Spirit is often described as the love relationship between the Father and the Son. You pray for the power of the Holy Spirit. Yes, He is a Person of the Holy Trinity, but also the relationship. But do not forsake good form and reverence. It flows from the relationship. Sometimes the form leads to the relationship, at other times the relationship produces better form. Both are needed.

Lord, You have truly revealed much of Yourself to me today. I am in awe and want to honor You even more that I naturally do. I actually see my relationship with You growing.

Now, Lord, I do offer myself to You ...

Maggie, I accept your offering. I know it seemed like all you did yesterday was pray. You are still missing the fact that your prayers are effective and that I am with you. It is still something

you think you have-to or should do. Like doing dishes or laundry. No joy. If one of your sons came through your door, how would you react?

It would be wonderful.

Would you feel obligated to talk to him?

No, it would come naturally – and I would gladly drop anything I was doing to spend time with him.

Exactly. Right now, I would appreciate your considering any prayer as speaking with one of your sons, or any dear friend or family member. Prayer is relationship. Even when your prayer is for another person or your country, think of it as you and I conspiring, huddled together, to do good for the object of your prayer. Sort of like planning a surprise party.

Today, as you prayed for your cousin, Maria, think of it as planning a surprise gift for her birthday. When you ask Me to hold her close, it is indeed a surprise gift for her. All the praying you did yesterday, they all had effects – though you could not see them.

Lord, we are back at that invisibility thing again.

Yes, but this is when your faith must kick in. What you can't see, you still believe. My love for you, My care and provision, all My gifts, graces, and blessings – most are invisible. Yet you are grateful. You know they are all there working for your good. You thank Me often. This is good.

But I think I still need one of Your attitude transplants about prayer.

Would you like one?

Yes, with all my heart. Please change the way I think of prayer.

That is what I am doing now. Prayer is like breathing. I am the air. Always there – sustaining your life. When one has had trouble breathing, and is finally healed, and breathing becomes easy again, they appreciate each breath much more. You have had your struggles with prayer for a long time. Now that it is not as labored, you need to enjoy it. But you often treat prayer as a breathing treatment in a hospital. It is not meant to be so. Consider yourself healed and breathe easily. Even if the air is

humid, and not as you would really like, does not affect that it is there, and helpful and good. **Now breathe freely.**

Lord, a song came to my mind just now: "With every breath I take, I want to worship You." Is prayer the same as worship?

It can and should be. It is union with me – the desire of your heart.

Thank You, Lord. I feel Your Presence, and it is the desire of my heart. I am in awe.

Stay there, it is good. I AM with you.

Dear Jesus, I come to You tonight repenting. It seems there is some hypocrisy within me. I claim to love serving You, but it must be on my terms. Yesterday at 2 PM, I had just gotten home from an appointment. I had not even caught my breath from climbing the stairs, when my grand-niece showed up wanting to bake cupcakes, since turning on their oven would make their house too hot.

She did ask a day or two ago if we could do that, and I agreed, but no special time or day was agreed on. I had – in my mind – already planned out my afternoon and evening. I had many things yet to do, and several messages on the computer to listen to – not to mention the programs I wanted to watch. My kitchen was a mess from the work I did the day before, and I certainly was not in the mood for baking cupcakes with an 11-year-old.

But I felt obligated as I had agreed to do it, and my attitude was sour. I cursed under my breath as I cleaned some counter space, realized that I needed to produce all the ingredients except the cake mixes, and eventually my attitude sweetened and we baked cupcakes. My oven did not make my house unbearably hot, the cupcakes turned out well, and I could finally focus on my own work.

In two more hours, I had finished. But I was completely exhausted, and my back was aching, and I was plotting in my mind what would happen if I did not do any more of my work, which would make my back hurt even more. So I consoled myself with some sweets, reclined in my chair in the living room, and turned on the TV. After a while, leaving the TV on, I did get up, and did some computer work. I was surprised that I could do it with the TV on, half-listening and still able to concentrate on my work.

I finally finished a little after 9 PM, glad that it was done, and proceeded to get to bed. Your Presence was wonderfully strong as I prayed, and I then went to sleep quickly. But then I had a disturbing dream.

In the dream, I was having to decide if another person – some lady – could move into my house. I already had an extra young man living here – other than those who rent my basement, and I would have to let this lady live upstairs in one of my two extra bedrooms, so what little privacy I still had would be gone. But she needed a place to live, and there were two people in the room pressuring me to let her come. I finally got upset with the ones bullying and sent them away angrily, and was left alone with the lady. I asked her what she could contribute to the already full household, and her reply did not impress me. I complained that I did not want another person who did not clean up after themselves – but in my heart I could not turn her away. I relented. I felt I was too weak to refuse her, and my mother even showed up trying to tell me that this was not a good idea. But I replied that everyone knew I would not be able to refuse her, and it felt like I lacked the courage to do so. Inside I felt having been taken advantage of, but did not know how to avoid it.

I then woke up realizing that I had the same feelings in the dream that I had in the afternoon. So now, I thought You gave me the dream to show me that there are parts of me that are in conflict. I do want to be of service, but do feel taken advantage of at times. I allow it – not out of a generous heart but from an attitude of weakness – not wanting to say "no." It seems to negate the good that I would do, and perhaps even my attitude with prayer is in the same category. A part of me has to say yes – and another part of me resents it and then, rather than the joy of doing good, I am left with a feeling of defeat and weakness. Lord, only You can sort this out.

Yes, Maggie, I can. Remember My agony in the garden. I also experienced exactly what you are describing. I wanted and chose to do My Father's Will. I had agreed to do this before I came to

the earth. This was My reason for coming. But the prospect – when it was imminent – was overwhelming. I had to choose – and the choice was harder than I expected. But I did choose – as you did as well. And eventually the grace kicked in, and things turned out OK.

This is why you have to <u>choose</u> joy. There are occasions when it is a difficult choice. But it is possible. In Scripture it says that, "for the joy set before Me, I endured the Cross." I actually chose it. You are not yet at the point of actually choosing something you may not want to do. That is the next step. Right now – it is not your choice, but what you feel you have-to do. It needs to become a choice.

I am answering your prayer to strengthen your will that you may better live your life according to My direction and purpose. For that, you first need to consult Me in these situations. Ask Me what I want you to do -- the grace and attitude will follow if you know you are doing My Will. Then choose to do it. Joy will come with the choice.

Did that help?

Yes, Lord, it did. Thank You.

Lord, here is the matter I want to consider: I heard one of my favorite authors say that the evil spirits our nation needs to fight are the same as the ancient gods that the Biblical Hebrews had to fight. But he says there is hope, because of the recent Supreme Court decisions, there is a crack in their power, and now You can come with Your power and glory, and the great revival can happen. In the past, this author was always telling us about the problems. Now, he offers some hope. I was glad to hear that, as I do appreciate his books and teachings.

Lord, I believe he and the other prophets are correct. But the big question is what can I do about all this? I pray, I listen, I do whatever good works You allow me to do, but still feel puny and insignificant as far as Your army is concerned. I gladly put on Your armor but need reassurance that it does any good.

I am your reassurance. Your relationship with Me is growing by leaps and bounds. You know much more clearly when I want you to do something, and you even ask Me if it really is My Will. Your desire is to be united to Me. You want to please Me. I am leading you, inspiring you, protecting you, and using you. As part of the protection,

I do not tell you what is still in the future. I prepare you a little at a time. Your prayers are effective. Keep them up. Whether it is formal or personal prayer, it is all reaching Me. Those prayers join with the prayers of many others and are the raw materials I use for the coming revival. They are also the weapons needed for this fight.

Remember Rosie the Riveter. During WWII, simple housewives learned to help build the weapons of the war. They did not go and shoot enemy soldiers, but what they contributed were essential to winning the war. It was a very big war. This one is even bigger. But not all My army is on the front lines at all times. I need the army of helpers that support and equip those on the front lines. Do you think I consider those who make uniforms, or prepare food, or other supplies for the soldiers are not fighting in the battle? Without them, the army would be ill-equipped and easily defeated.

But this war is different, in that much of the fight is invisible. Not flesh and blood, but powers and principalities. So, your prayers and declarations equip the angel armies, as well as those you hear about who are fighting the fight in a more visible way. The prophets, apostles, pastors, evangelists, and teachers need your support. There are times I use you in one of these roles on a smaller scale. You will not necessarily appear in the news, but your role is still just as important. This fight is so big, that anyone willing to participate will have plenty to do.

You have been doing this ever since you started getting up to pray daily. Your daily Mass and Rosaries are also more effective than you realize. You come to Me, and I come to you. It is union.

It is love. It is good. Do not fear that you are not doing enough. Even soldiers on the front lines have to eat and sleep, and sometimes have some sort of recreation.

In My army, there is also joy. You are encouraged to enjoy the things I give you. You worry that you are not constantly aware of Me. There will come a time when that will happen, but it is not yet. Your awareness of Me is growing, but I do not take it as an insult when you are totally absorbed in some other activity. I provide those activities in your life for good reasons.

Recently, you have experienced great peace, and at other times great turmoil. When you had peace, you realized it was My gift to you. When you had turmoil with the illnesses of your friends, you came to Me with their problems and I helped you encourage them. I inspired you to do good for your family. I even provided things you could not have had. I am with you always.

Right now, you feel My Presence. But even when you do not, I am there. My love sustains and envelops you. Your love delights Me. Not just your love for Me, but also for those I put in your path. Is that reassurance enough?

Yes, Lord, I get the message. I need to chill out and keep doing whatever next good thing I can.

Lord, thank You for all the help You give us. I have someone coming to help me clean today, and I am so glad. That is all that is going on in my life, how about Yours?

Heaven is great. You will like it here. But I see and care about the things of earth as well. There, I see both the good and the evil. I rejoice in the goodness and kindness of My people, just as you do. I am saddened by the evil and thoughtlessness of others as well.

I do many things no-one notices. My creation is not yet complete. I continue to create new and beautiful parts of the world. Like each new baby, it is with great love that I bring them forth.

Even the new life in the animals, is beautiful to see. Sunrises and sunsets are My artwork.

Do not focus on sickness and the evil in the world. There is much good to see if you open your eyes and mind to it. I continue to work on big things as well as the little concerns you have. There is a whole universe out there that most people have very little knowledge of.

There are many new things you can still learn and experience. Yes, awe and wonder are good. Regardless of the political situations, or the troubles you face, I have it all in control. You may not be able to control as much as you would like, but I do have a better plan, and as you get older and wiser, you see how My plans work better than what you expect.

I make beautiful things out of the greatest disasters. Remember the tree with the broken branch that was barely hanging on? I healed the break, and the branch flowered even more beautifully than the ones that never broke. And it was close enough to the ground that you could see the beauty of those flowers.

I do that with many situations. The sin of Adam and Eve resulted in My coming to earth. My Passion and Death led to Resurrection. My love cannot be extinguished. It is always there for you and everyone. It is good that you want to remain open and listening to Me. You can be content in My Presence.

Lord, I needed to get my mind on better things than I have been engulfed in. Thank You.

I know your needs as well as your desires. I am delighted to fulfill some of them. Not all. But many. And as you continue to come to Me, you also meet some of My desires. You are made in My image. We desire a lot of the same things. It is good.

Lord, I heard another message last night, and it seemed to confirm what You were telling me in prayer, It was all about Your great goodness, and how we tend to only attribute disasters to You.

Yes, I have been telling you that your recounting your day to Me is not as silly as you had thought. Yes, I know all that happened, I was with you through it all, but just as you delight in My revealing Myself to you in your time of prayer, when you tell Me all about your day, you are revealing yourself to Me. It is a part of a good friendship to tell one another about the things that happen or are on your heart. It enhances the relationship.

Even retelling old experiences between friends is delightful. When two friends talk, both are blessed. So it is with you and Me. I bless you by letting you see and understand Me better, and I am blessed by your revealing your thoughts and actions of the day.

I also appreciate it when you tell Me or ask Me about what is coming up in your life. It is not that I don't know it already, but that you are wanting to discuss things with Me. This is a loving relationship. It is what My heart and your heart has longed for. It is another aspect of the total union you demanded so long ago.

I did demand it, didn't I? But I thought I was out of line speaking to You that way. I am so glad that You were not offended. In fact, I believe You were amused, and delighted to begin to meet that demand. I certainly am grateful that You took it seriously. And now that I can see that it is happening, I am even more grateful.

I feel such tremendous blessing in having this relationship with You. I'm still not too good at it, but You are teaching me. Many years ago, at a retreat I was told about spiritual marriage with You. I immediately desired it but thought it unlikely that I would ever experience it. Yet at that same retreat, You proposed it, and I was led to say a resounding "Yes!" Thank You ever so much. I was expecting to wait tables at the Marriage Supper of the Lamb but found myself being the bride. Your goodness and kindness are beyond what we can even imagine.

And there is more to come. I am not finished with you yet. Enjoy the blessings and remember My love and care as you encounter difficulties. There is nothing you cannot come to Me with. Let's keep this relationship vibrant and close. I am with you.

Lord, You are wonderful

Thank You, that Your blessings are so obvious to me, and that I do belong to You. Help me to keep listening and learning. Keep me ever closer to You and let me be a pleasure in Your sight and a credit to Your Name. Lord, You have been so good to me, could I do something good to You?

As you do good to others, you are doing good to Me. Keep praying and caring. Remember the glove parable? How I am the hand inside and you are My glove that touches others as they have needs. They are blessed in My work through you, but you have My touch within you. Now think of the One who wears the glove. Does not a glove give benefits to the wearer, also? As a glove, you get My hand and touch within you, but I also get your warmth and comfort.

Wow, Lord, I was so impressed with the honor of being used in other people's lives and having such close contact with You, that I never even considered that You would have any benefit from my functioning as Your glove. One does not wear a glove without it having some benefit for the wearer. The thought that my being available to You for whatever You desire, has not entered into my mind before.

You are delighted to be used by Me in people's lives. But I am delighted to be able to help others through you as well. So now we are looking at a "three-way street." That is not easily imagined. Perhaps we need to think in terms of three dimensions instead. Length, width, and height. All three work together for the benefit of all.

The one being touched, the glove on the outside that actually touches, and is filled on the inside by the One doing the work that needs to be done. I, on the inside, am blessed and delighted to be able to accomplish what I desire (My Will), you are blessed though intimate contact both with Me and with all those that are helped through you. And those being loved and helped are also getting the benefit of your touch as well as Mine.

I supply the strength as well as the direction of the action. You are the channel through which I can reach another person. And that person receives the benefit of both your care and Mine. You are blessed from both the outside and the inside. It is good, very good.

Lord, I am in awe of You.

I received a call from a mother of a successful married daughter, and she asked me to pray for her daughter that she and her husband would be willing to have children. Lord, this is exactly what You put on my heart some time ago, that You would move on the hearts of our young people that they should welcome new life and not be reluctant to embrace parenthood. There are so many good and able couples who have believed the lie that children are a burden rather than a blessing. Lord, send the convicting power of Your Holy Spirit to change their minds and hearts, that they would be able to generously give of their time and energy to bring forth another generation. Thank You.

Lord, I also ask that as a part of this coming revival, You bring lots of new life, I mean babies, into the world. Let there be a desire once again for having and caring for families. I believe You desire this even more than I do.

I do. It is not only evil and corruption that I want to eradicate, but the attitudes of this society that are so contrary to My heart. Many will need attitude transplants. I did it for you, and I can and will do it for many others.

Lord, I want to thank You for teaching me through the lives of others. You have shown me Beauty in people's lives even when they have lost much of the abilities they once had. Help me to be a blessing to others even when I can no longer serve them the way I would like to.

This is what you are doing now. You are mostly blind and often lame, but you serve Me and bless others. I do not need perfect bodies and minds, but willing spirits and loving hearts. These

can grow as bodies and minds deteriorate. Yes, I can and do heal. I did come that you might have life and have it more abundantly.

But the world's definition of abundance and Mine are different. You have begun to see what I consider important. Keep looking for My ways and thoughts. See the beauty of the peace I give through adversity. The gentleness of one who has experienced the need of others, the goodness of those who earnestly desire to help, the patience of those who have learned My ways. It is good fruit that I look for. The Fruit of the Spirit.

Fame, fortune, physical beauty, they are good for a season, but do not last. But I look for good fruit, not just the leaves. Remember the fig tree, it had leaves, but no fruit.

Lord Jesus, this morning, You are showing me that pride is raising its ugly head. I see it through Your grace, and I do thank You for that grace. But I don't know how to get rid of it. I do repent, but it seems I need much help to root it out of my soul.

Are you asking for that help, or are you planning to try to do it yourself?

Not only am I asking, but I am also begging.

You know that the antidote to pride is humility.

Yes, and I have not been great friends with that virtue.

It is not an easy one to befriend. But look to Me in the Scriptures. You do not find pride in My miracles, in My prayer life, in My care for others. Come unto Me and learn from Me for I am meek and humble of heart. I knew I was following My Father's direction at all times. I was happy to give Him credit. Humility is not denying the gifts that you have but realizing that they are actually gifts.

I did not do great things to show off that I was great, but because My Father sent Me to do those things, and I saw Him doing those things. You admire your mother's selflessness in how she helped your father navigate when he could no longer see well enough to drive without her help. Yet, she did not think it was a

great thing, she simply saw the need to do so. It was simply who she was.

You are struggling with doing good, but then seeking to take credit for your goodness. Yet you know that the reason you do the good, is that you need to do it. You have an enemy that delights in sharing his greatest vice. It was his pride that hurled him out of heaven. It only benefits him to have you infected with the same vice.

When you see a point of pride in your life, it is not a time for you to wallow in guilt or cease doing the good you seem to be proud of, but a time to resist the devil and draw near to Me. I do provide the help you need. And besides, the union both you and I desire will be enhanced.

Humility is not the same as humiliation. It is not denying your gifts but realizing that those gifts are given for good reasons. So, you found yourself subtly bragging about getting up during the night to pray. Yes, that was a point of pride. But the remedy is not to stop getting up to pray but realizing that it simply works for you. Repent of the bragging, but do not give up praying at night. It is My gift to you to be able to wake up enough to engage in prayer. Rejoice in the gift and avoid drawing attention to it. Even realizing that the subtle bragging is wrong is a gift.

You have known for years that when I convict you of sin, I also provide the grace and strength to overcome it. You now have that strength and grace. Gratitude is also a good antidote for pride. You do thank Me often for waking you for prayer. Your motives are not the problem. Your attitude does need some help. Consider this a transplant. Now go back to sleep at peace. My love for you is much greater than you can imagine.

Thank You so much, Lord.

Dear Jesus, today is Thanksgiving Day. And I have so much to thank You for. Big things as well as little things. I don't even know if the little things are so little. Thank You that though I had a lot of pain when I went to bed, it is not bothering me now. Thank You most of all for belonging. That I belong to You, to my family, to this marvelous country.

It is good to be grateful. It is good that this country sets a day aside for gratitude. It is still a marvelous country as you put it. Despite all the problems, it still belongs to Me, and I will bring it back. Your book, will also help. There is a lot of work that went into it, and I know you are grateful that it is just about done, but I, too, am grateful that you and all who helped you did such a work. I also give thanks.

I thank My Father for each soul that chooses to love. Yes, I thank My Father for you and all the marvelous people in your life. And, yes, they are marvelous. Like the country, they may have some issues, but down deep there is much good. I see the good. I forgive the bad. I heal the hurts. I love My people. Yes, you do belong to Me. And I belong to you. It is good.

Dear Jesus, thank You for Your love and care. It was a good day yesterday, ending with a couple of hours of conversation and math with my grand-nephew. He is almost 14, and it has become enjoyable to spend time with him. Lord, thank You that I enjoy talking with teenagers.

See, here is another way you and I are alike. I also enjoy talking with those that others may find annoying. For Me it was tax collectors and sinners. Any group of people who are only thought of as a group, rather than individuals, can easily get overlooked or disliked. It was the same in My day. "Can anything good come out of Nazareth?"

Yes, many times I have been surprised that I really liked someone I would never have thought of associating with because they appeared to be associated with a group I would not enjoy.

It is inevitable to group people and even animals or objects, but assuming they are all alike especially with a bad trait, is how prejudices are formed. Pit bulls are considered vicious and unde-

sirable. Yet many have found great joy and affection for their pit bulls and found them gentle and faithful animals. It is easy to group people or animals, or things, but takes time to get to know details that may not fit the grouping. The current culture is very guilty of this. Do not be deceived into adopting this flaw. Take the time to get to know the good I have placed in each person. I do. Then you can build on that and encourage growth in goodness. It is worth the time.

As You have done with me. Thank You.

Dear Jesus, thank You that You answered our prayers for my sister. Thank You also that the day went well yesterday. I was able to stay on the bike for seven minutes, and today I hope to try for eight. There were no cramps, but my body was quite achy most of the night. I seem to be better now, so I thank You. I also think a big package will arrive this week, so please let there be someone available to bring them in. I also hope to put away some decorations this week. I will need help with that as well.

Maggie, it is good. You are relying on Me more, and things are getting done without worry or stress. My peace is again upon you. You felt My Presence last night when you prayed. It is good that you have begun to exercise a bit and eat more responsibly. I will bless these efforts. Good habits are still good. Just because they have become habits that are done without much thought, they are still effective. You can please your God without having to try as hard when goodness becomes a habit. In fact, there is much freedom in having good habits. When goodness becomes effortless, there is freedom and room for joy.

Lord, there You go again, sneaking joy in my life. Thank You.

Come, Holy Spirit, I seem to have trouble thinking or praying right now.

That is why you have a spiritual language.

OK, I'll try that. _____

It seems intercession is the order of this day. I thank You for all the people in my life past and present. You have truly blessed me throughout my life with wonderful people who loved and taught me. Help me be one such wonderful person in the lives of others.

I am doing that through your writing as well as your teaching and even your conversations with others. Now let My peace permeate your being.

Thank You, Lord. It is so good to be enveloped in Your love and peace.

In the evening, Rosemary called to let me know that Fr. Ousley is in the hospital having had a TIA. She asked that I call some people to ask for prayers, and I called several Ladies of Charity, and everyone in my prayer group. I asked everyone to pray for Fr. Ousley. So out of his need, I was able to spread Your love and care, and receive it as well.

Lord, I do pray for Fr. Ousley. I ask that You wrap Your loving arms around him, hold him close, and heal him. Bring him back to us as soon as possible, as he has truly been a blessing to us. Also, keep his family calm and reassure them of Your Presence and care. Thank You for all they do for us.

This is what love is supposed to be. Even a need is to bring people together. My love touched many souls last night just because you called and asked them to pray. And in turn, you were touched by each person you called. It is good.

My love is to be spread like that. So often people wonder why I allow difficulties into people's lives. Here is a case where it brought good fruit. I do not send adversity, but it can be a springboard for much good. And, yes, all those prayers are answered. Not only that, but each one who prays, is also able to feel My love and care.

Like I said, You are awesome.

In our small groups at church, we had been praying for a young mother who was in danger of losing her pregnancy, and another young lady who was missing. Both prayers were wonderfully answered. The missing girl had been abducted, but was found alive, and the pregnancy stabilized. One of our priests was also having health problems, and I was praying for him.

Lord, thank You for the answers to our prayers. Your goodness is so wonderful. Please help our priest stay well. He has gone through a lot lately.

Many of My closest friends have gone through a lot lately. But none of it is wasted. In the sufferings and difficulties, there is the seed of growth and redemption. Not just for the one suffering, but for many others as well. Remember that I take whatever you offer Me, and fashion a blessing for you or someone that needs it. I have plans in place for every situation.

Back when Adam sinned, I already had redemption planned. Fear not. Keep trusting Me and see what I do. I can handle major world events as well as that small pain in your toe. Nothing is too big or too small. Do keep asking. I use your prayers to involve you in My work. You are My partner in the things I do. Remember that this is not the only part of life.

There is eternal life as well. What does not get resolved here, will be resolved there. Justice and mercy work together and I know how and when and where to apply them. You stay close to Me. I will help you fight your battles, and you will help Me fight Mine. Together, we cannot lose.

When one of our past prayer group members died, I prayed:
Please give him a big hug for me. As well as all our other prayer group people on Your side of eternity.

Funny how that does not sound good. "Your side of eternity" sounds like this side of eternity is not Yours as well. But I suppose You know what I mean.

I do, and I do not get offended by such words. There is a division between earthly life and eternal life. Many of those you know and love have crossed over. This week is all about how I crossed over as well. At the beginning of Lent, you are reminded that you will also cross over at some time. Next Sunday you will be reminded that the other side is worth all the pains and difficulties of this side. But until I am ready to receive you there, you have things to do here. I have all the plans. They are good.

Thank You, Lord.

Lord, I am listening, I really need to hear Your voice.

Fear not! I have not stopped speaking to you. You have gone through some difficult health issues and are now on the mend. As your strength returns, you will see more good works to walk in. I have prepared many for you. Keep doing what you can. Keep looking and listening for My directions. Do not pay too much attention to whether or not you want to do what is set before you. Do it anyway. I appreciate obedience even if it is half-hearted. But soon it will become a pleasure, as you realize how you have the power to please your God. Let My love guide you through this day.

Heavenly Father, thank You for Fathering me. It is such a privilege to be Your child. Your love for me is indeed more than I can understand, but it is something I have felt and enjoyed and am grateful for. I also thank You for all the other fathers that have been in my life. You do not leave us orphans. You provide us with fathers even when our natural fathers cannot meet our needs. I thank You for all the priests that have fathered me, and there have been many. And I pray for those that are yet to come into my life.

You have now found another way to please your God. Not too many of My children are grateful for My Fatherhood. But then, not all that many children really are grateful for their fathers. There is a reason some jobs are called thankless. Many times, parenthood is that way. But we do these jobs regardless of benefits. There are benefits, but sometimes they are only realized long after the service. Goodness and generosity are often overlooked, but there is a heaven where it all works out.

I suppose that is one of the ways we can have a bit of heaven on earth, by being grateful.

It is indeed. When you are grateful, there is no room for any other negative thoughts and feelings. It is a heavenly part of earthly life.

And I do thank You for teaching me this.

Lord, You have given me great rest the past few nights. This morning was the first time I remember recently that I did not fight getting up and coming to You due to overwhelming fatigue. Thank You. I came at the first thought that perhaps You were calling me. I remember when I first started coming to You around 3:00 AM, how I was often so grateful and amazed that You woke me up just at the exact time. Does that count as a "first love"? And are You rekindling my "first love" for You? If so, I certainly thank You.

Yes, I am doing a new thing in you. Knowledge of Me is traveling from your head to your heart. You have recently heard that there is a higher level you need to start living in. Embrace it. Notice the changes and accept them with joy. Right now, you are feeling My Presence in a very strong way. That is also My generous gift to you. I am gently guiding you to higher ground. The past two days, you had a few specific goals to accomplish, and you did them. You have two for today. I will help you. Rejoice with Me when each is done.

Thank You, Lord. I do appreciate clear directions. You are providing them.

And I am affirming them with My Presence and peace. It is not only your prayers that I hear and answer, but all the prayers that you have accepted that were prayed over you by My friends. Whether in person or over the airwaves, I have blessed you with powerful prayers. They also count. I answer prayer. Yours and also those of others.

Do not be stingy with your prayers. Lavish them on others. Receive them when they are offered for you as precious jewels, knowing that I hear and answer. Do you feel the higher ground I have taken you to? Before, when others prayed for you, your reaction was more of a hope than a faith, now it will begin to change into an assurance. This is very good. You are seeing a much bigger picture.

Lord, when I heard in the teachings recently that we need to go to a higher ground, I had thought it was something that depended on me. I wondered how I can do that. But it is You who are taking me there, and I had nothing to strive for or achieve. Thank You ever so much. Now I see why You have to take the controls in our lives. When we think we are in control, not only do we mess it up, but it takes much more work and effort and uncertainty than when we allow You to do things. You must increase, and I must decrease. Please keep reminding me.

I can do that.

Lord, how are You doing? The world still seems to be falling apart, yet You have been so lovingly helping us.

I am still in charge. When on the earth, I did get tired and grateful for the care of those who loved Me. Now I am still grateful for the love and care of all who love Me, but the fatigue and pains of earthly life do not affect Me. Your love and care for others is as precious to Me as if it was directly given to Me. They still get weary and need many things, and I am delighted that you

can be there to do what I would gladly do in the flesh. **You are My gloves. I work inside, but it is you that are visible, and My strength comes through you. And, yes, I did cleanse and re-fill you through the night just as you asked.**

Thank You, Lord. It is so great to be of service.

Lord, I thank You for being my God. Thank You that You are always available. That I can rest in Your loving arms any time. That You listen to and answer my prayers. That I have all I need and much more. That You have given me great friends and family, and gifts and blessings beyond measure.

It is good to be thankful. Have you ever considered that I, too, am thankful? I am thankful for every soul that seeks Me. That I can work through each one to accomplish My Father's Will. That I can have companions not only in heaven, but here on earth as well. That there is still much good in this fallen world, and that goodness still overcomes evil. I am thankful for your trusting Me and relying on Me for so much more than you ever did. You give joy to your God.

Lord, that is one of the greatest things I am thankful for. That I can actually give You, the Father, and the Holy Spirit joy. It is a thought so far beyond my comprehension. But I am truly grateful.

Chapter 8

Gentleness

Father, I thank You that You have given me such wonderful family and friends. You have brought me back to seeking Your Will even when I was not writing, but now it seems much more possible to know what You desire of me.

You had to go through the struggles to become stronger. In your uncertainties. Your desires for the communication with Me to once again be clear and active grew. You had to overcome what you thought was no longer possible. With Me there are always possibilities. There is a reason for aging and all the diminishments that come with it. You realize how much you need Me. You cannot do everything you used to be able to do. You see that there is much less you can control. But dependence on Me, when perfected, is beautiful and powerful. You see Me working through you – even through your infirmities – and you are grateful realizing that you are not doing everything on your own power. I waste nothing.

Give Me your pains, your frustrations, your desires, your successes and failures. I see them all. You used to think you were helping Me in following Me. Now you see that it is a partnership where I do most of what is needed. But you are and always will be Mine.

Dear Jesus, thank You for another good prayer during the night. When I went back to bed, You did not stop talking to me. I even invented a new word. I realized that I offered myself to You, and You accepted. That is why You said that I am Yours. As an alien in this country long ago, being accepted and belonging are very precious to me. But then I also realized that You offered Yourself to me, and I accepted. So, the relationship between You and me is "acceptional." I know it is not a real word, but I like it.

Yesterday You showed me ever so gently that there was a root of pride in something I said. Please help me to remove this. I do repent and am grateful that You did not point it out to me to shame me, but to improve me. Even Your rebuke is wonderful as it brings the desire to improve. Thank You.

Maggie, you are once again alert to My correction. It is not meant to tear you down, but simply to perfect you. I do gladly forgive.

Lord, Your Presence is strong upon me.

It is to assure you that your awareness of My correction is growth. It is producing gratitude and joy. I am increasing your humility. I am growing it within you.

You have a hard job ahead of You.

I am up to the challenge.

Dear Jesus, thank You so much for Your gentleness and forgiveness. Last night You taught me that our sins are like ticks. We might not even see them, but if You or someone else does, and removes them, we are grateful. Then ticks must be destroyed so they cannot get on someone else. But if they attach themselves to us, bite us, suck out our blood, then the removal can be painful, and the spot needs to be disinfected and the diseases they carry need to be monitored and treated if necessary.

Confession, penance, and awareness, as well as avoiding places where sin can be found are the remedies. Often, we are not able to remove a tick by ourselves, we need Someone else to see it and destroy it.

Lord, You have so much to deal with. I am sure Your heart is breaking for the disasters and troubles Your people are enduring. You endure it all with them. Let me soothe Your aching hands and feet – maybe rub Your back, caress Your face, wipe away Your tears. You do that for us, could we do that for You?

As you do it for each other, you do it for Me. The least of My brethren are everywhere. Sometimes they look like they would not be considered the least. But all are needy. When you are kind to anyone, you are soothing My aching hands and feet. Your gifts to others rub My back and kiss My face. Even if they don't thank you, I do. My love puts you in their path.

When you are on the receiving end of someone else doing things for you, learn from Me as to how to accept ministry graciously. I received Mary Magdalene's perfume, Veronica's veil, John's head on My chest. None of that embarrassed Me. I ate meals others prepared, even invited Myself to Zacchaeus' house, received Mary's devotion and Martha's service. And then there is My Mother – how much she did for Me. And all I learned from my earthly father, Joseph.

All were gifts from My Heavenly Father. You are also a gift of My Heavenly Father, as are all those who help you along the way. Humility is not thinking that you are less or worse than you want to think of yourself. It is the truth that you are valued but also in need. I helped many, but many also helped Me. I accepted both the good and the bad.

Come unto Me, learn from Me. As I hold you close, you also hold Me close. As I come to you, you also come to Me. It is good. Let us all rejoice and be glad. Yes, there is trouble and pain and terrible things, but there is infinite goodness as well. It

is good to reflect on the positive when the negative seems to be overwhelming.

Lord, I cannot begin to thank You enough. Do hold me and let me hold on to You.

Help me to get everything done that I need to do. Thank You that right now everything is on track.

I am giving you the strength you need. But I am also giving you the rest in between spurts of activity. It is good to keep pushing yourself, but I want you to do so in small increments. As you see, you are able to do things now that you would have left undone. And you remembered to pray at times when you normally do not.

Thank You, Lord.

Dear Jesus, thank You for another way of interceding for the people in my life. I remembered how a past retreat director taught me to pray for at least 50 people by mentioning them by name and then following with a familiar prayer. We often pray for each state of the United States this way, as well as for each part of the government. I started praying for individual people the way we pray for each state. I continued praying, "I plead the blood of Jesus for "_____" and adding another prayer. I don't know how many more people I prayed for this way, but I think I went through as many friends and family members as I could think of, until I fell asleep. Thank You for a new (to me) form of prayer.

And you felt My approval and that it was an effective way to bring your loved ones to Me. It is a good way to bring people to Me. Intercession is important. But you have also been heavy-laden about particular people in your life, and this method of prayer seemed to relieve that. I have not been sending you back to bed these nights because your prayers are lacking due to fatigue,

but because I want to love away your cares. When you come to me in the dark of night, it is not only you trying to reach Me, but I am also reaching out to you.

I know your heart's needs. Lately, it has not been your mind that needed attention, as when I reveal a truth to you, but your heart has been aching for various reasons. As you come to Me, I see more than what you write. I see body, soul, and spirit. The teachings will be back, but for a while, the heart needs attention. Bringing your loved ones to Me this way relieved your heart a bit. I want you to be able to not only care for others, but to leave your cares for them with Me. Let Me take the burden off of you. This is a way to take My yoke upon you.

Lord, I thank You. I feel Your kindness and gentleness in caring for those I love, but even more for the way You are loving me. I want to just hold on to You and just cry. But I don't like crying, and yet You know how I feel. When I go back to bed and pull the covers over me as if they were Your arms enfolding me, I often feel consoled, or calmed, or even energized. You supply my needs in marvelous ways. In fact, You supply my needs when I don't even know I have those needs.

The lives of others, the news you hear, even your own physical condition all affect you. They affect Me as well. As you feel Me holding you, I also feel you holding Me. I console you, and you console Me. It is an important part of the relationship. It is what friends and spouses do for and with each other. Do not be ashamed of being needy. Just as you love meeting the needs of others, so do I. My love for you sees your needs before you do.

You do this for others as well. And as you do so, you are doing it for Me. My needs are also met. Yes, I do have needs. You are made in My image and likeness. What you do for others, you do for Me. But right now, it is time to rest a bit, and let all these thoughts wait for another time. Do feel My arms around you. I am here.

Thank You, Lord.

On the first day of the year:

Dear Jesus, thank You that You are the first One I can say Happy New Year to.

Lord, I have long pauses lately when I come to You. It seems like I don't know how to continue. Holy Spirit, I need Your help. I am stuck. Perhaps I need to pray in the Spirit until You bring another topic to my mind.

The end of a year and the beginning of a new one is a time to pause. It is a time to take inventory. What went well, what did not, and how to proceed. Yet, I have been telling you not to "grade" your life, so it is natural that you are reluctant to indulge in such matters. You did not make any New Year's resolutions. Why not?

They seem pretty useless. They are often abandoned very quickly. I thought about needing to exercise more, but unless You direct my actions, I will fail.

Fear of failure is still an issue.

I suppose so.

And what is the remedy for any fear?

Your love. Did I lose track of Your love, and allow fear to take over?

You were heading in that direction.

But yesterday You touched me so gently and kindly that I could hardly contain the joy and peace. How did it change so quickly?

It had help. Focusing on difficulties has a way of changing the atmosphere.

But You provided much more positive things to dwell on.

True, but you let your guard down. Negative thoughts and feelings were creeping in. Little, unnoticeable irritations piled up and counteracted any joy or peace.

I see. Is there a way to guard against all this?

Of course, there is. I am the Way.

I suppose I need to learn how to draw nearer to You when I find myself having negative thoughts or feelings.

It is not easy when these thoughts and feelings come in so imperceptibly. You need to rely on My guidance on a regular basis.

I will need lots of help.

I know. It is My plan that you should need My help. My desire is that all of your life would be so intertwined with My help and guidance that you would not even conceive of doing anything without Me.

Union?

Exactly. It is possible. But it is not automatic.

Warfare?

Yes, but you have the armor and are not alone.

You think of everything.

Omniscience has its privileges.

You did it again. Brought a smile to our conversation when it was pretty intense. Thank You.

I am also smiling. It will be a good year.

Even when we find ourselves in our own failures, the Lord treats us with His truth so gently;

Lord Jesus, I come to You upset that I know what I should be doing but I have not been doing it. My eating the past few days has been destructive of my own body. I did not want to face You about it, and for the past two hours have been avoiding coming to You with my partial remorse. Partial because I know I am likely to keep failing in this area if I do not seriously repent, but not really wanting to repent on my own. I thought if I came to You, You would simply love me, and I would not change. I know it is to You that I need to come to. So here I am. The way I have been eating is destructive. You know it, I know it, and I know I should and could do much better.

The eating is simply an outward sign of another issue.

You are quite right, Lord. It is harder to face that one.

Are you willing to name it?

I suppose I must. It is a resentment and rebellion for being alone.

And why is that so bad?

Because it is not true. I am not alone at all. You are with Me, in me. But why does that not satisfy me? I think it should, but it does not. Even admitting that makes me ashamed. I want to be satisfied with Your love and companionship, but I desperately seek what I do not have. I did not want to give in to loneliness, but it snuck up on me.

So, the root sin is dissatisfaction.

I suppose so.

But you thought you needed to repent of wrong eating.

No wonder I could not sleep. So how do I repent of this sin? And how do I avoid it?

Let's take it one step at a time. Are you now ready to repent of dissatisfaction, resentment, and rebellion?

Absolutely. Lord, I am truly sorry. I do repent. Please forgive me.

I do forgive you. Now, do you have any thoughts of how to avoid all these things?

I suppose gratitude must be a part of it. But there must be more to it than that.

There is. One step has already been taken. Identifying it. You must now be alert to the beginnings of your dissatisfaction. Yesterday you named it disappointment. They have the same root. You want something a particular way but cannot have it. On the surface you seem to handle it well, but underneath, it eats away at you. Then it surfaces when no-one is looking and self-destructive behavior results. Eve had a similar problem. She was dissatisfied with not being allowed to eat of the forbidden fruit.

Am I not accepting my state in life? My widowhood? My children not being nearby? After all these years?

There is some of that. Have you ever expressed gratitude for these things?

How can I be grateful for things I think are painful?

Have you not seen benefits from other painful things? Like your blindness?

I have sort-of seen them, but I still wish I could see well.

Can you trust Me to bring greater good out of what you have than what you wish for?

Well, when You put it that way, I suppose I can. I do believe You want only the best for me. And if I must be mostly blind, and alone, You see a much bigger picture than I do.

This does not mean that I want you to be blind or alone forever. You are allowed to have desires that do not match your current situation. You can ask, seek, and knock. But I can offer you better than what you ask for. It is My Will that you need to seek. It is My Presence you need to desire when you knock. You have asked and I have given you more than you even desired. You have sought Me and found Me. You have knocked, and the door has been open to you. I am always available to you.

Lord, now I really repent. It is You I have offended by my ingratitude. I do thank You for setting me apart for You. I can come closer to You by being alone. I just need to do that instead of resenting my situation. I need to rely on You so much more than I do. Please help me.

I am glad to do so.

Lord, I need to hear from You. You have treated me tenderly for some time now, and I do appreciate it. Pain has been intense at times, and fatigue as well. But it all leaves when I am in Your Presence. Especially when You speak to me.

And I do speak to you. But I am doing more than just speaking. You are more aware of My gentle touch and know I am here with you. It is the difference between talking to Me over the phone, long distance, vs. living together. I am not far off, but with you. When you feel My peace, or love, or joy, it is because I am here.

I am here even when you do not feel these things, but you appreciate and welcome My Presence whenever you become aware of it. Right now, it is mostly at night. But it is also happening at times during the day. It is good. It is the union you and I have longed for.

Your times of prayer are not limited to the amount of time you type. Do not think that because these times at night have become shorter that you are cheating Me. When you curl up with your covers wrapped around you and think of them as My arms enfolding you, that is also union. What you have longed for and sought for so long is happening. Do not doubt it.

Lord, I cannot thank You enough. I now gladly go back and have You wrap Your arms around me.

Thank You for Your patience with me.

Did you feel like a spectator in your life yesterday?

No, Lord, I think I was living it.

This is an occasion to rejoice.

Yes, Lord, You are right. You continue to heal me even when it is not physical. Though I certainly would not mind some more physical healing. I'm not complaining, You see, at least I'm trying not to.

Yes, I see. I am working from the inside out. If I just worked on the outside, the inner work would not be as effective. I do not work the same way with everyone. Your needs are different from the ones you see at healing services. You know I can and do heal. I do not need to convince you. But the healing you are receiving is deep inside.

Sometimes the pain inside is greater than the outward pain. I know. I have experienced both. I have healed both. Remember how you were once afraid to love Me because you thought that anything that hurt Me would hurt you as well? It also goes the other way. Since I love you, anything that hurts you, I also feel. But anything that gives you joy, that also makes Me rejoice.

That is why your contentment is so precious to Me. I have suffered through your doubts, your frenzy, your uncertainties for so long. It is so good to see you at peace. No more striving to be accepted. Being able to relax in My arms. It is good.

Yes, Lord, it is good indeed. Thank You for all Your work. And the loving gentleness with which You have done it. I am truly blessed. Help me to spread this blessing to others.

That is what I am doing through your writing. It works.

I do thank You.

After three days in the hospital:

Lord, most of all, I thank You that You were right there with me through it all. I thought I would pray a lot more than I did, but I did know that You were with me, and that each person who helped me was doing it because Your love was coming through them. The gentleness with which I was treated originated in You. I knew that though I was not praying much, there were many people praying for me, and I was surrounded by Your love. And that love continues here at home.

Lord, I have talked long enough. I need to listen now and hear Your voice.

Maggie, most people dread hospital visits, but I have given you the grace to feel My love through such situations. Yes, I was there with you through each moment just as much as I am with you now. And I am not leaving. I will strengthen you and help you with all that needs to be done. This will be a day of calm but sure strengthening. Rest as you need to but be assured that I am with you every moment. Now go back to bed and feel My loving arms around you.

Thank You, Lord.

Dear Jesus, Thank You for Your tender love. We were told yesterday that we either are running away from You or running to You. I want to be one who runs to You. Yet, there are many times I seem to be doing the opposite.

You have lots of help to run away: the world, the flesh, and the devil. But you also have lots of help to run to Me: Father, Son, Holy Spirit, angels, and Saints. I never let you get too far away. Isn't it good that I can be everywhere?

True. I have no place to run. And in my condition, I cannot run at all. Thank You for lightening up my perspective. I have let my flesh weigh me down. I'm sure the world and the devil also are in attack mode. Thank You that You do refresh me.

Please come with all Your gifts, graces, and blessings. We all really need everything You give us. And during this time of year, as we contemplate Your Passion and Death, we want to soothe Your pains as well. You are aware of all the hurts, struggles, tragedies, and wickedness in the whole world. Let us be a bit of comfort to You. Your love for us is beyond measure. Let us return some of that to You.

I am definitely open to Your plans whether or not mine get done.

It is time to lighten up again. As you go through the day, I want you to pause after each task, no matter how small, and celebrate with Me. Today is to be a joy with small duties well-done.

Lord just that gentle care and love, already lightened my disposition. Thank You that You want to be a part of the entire day. I suppose You always have, but it just really touched my heart now.

Let's make it a day of gentleness. Nothing really special or of great importance, but continual communion.

It sounds wonderful. I will rely on Your strength and direction.

Dear Jesus, it seems that for every step forward, I take several steps back.

It is time to turn around. Rather than wallow in guilt, making yourself more miserable, turn around and run to My open arms, ready to receive you, clean you up, and guide you out of the mud pit where you have been residing for the past several hours.

You are absolutely right and far more gracious than I deserve. Thank You for taking charge. I did not even know how to approach You.

I saw that. Turning around is not so difficult.

Especially when there are loving arms ready to welcome me. Lord, I do turn around. I make no promises, You see my heart and that I don't want to fall into that pit again. I do take Your hand, and gratefully stay still so You can clean me up.

Good, now go and sin no more.

Lord, You have been so gracious and gentle with me, and all our little groups. You handle us with such care, and continually encourage us. Let us truly be the mature sons and daughters You want us to be. No longer little children, though ready to receive Your goodness as little children, but mature and capable heirs of Your Kingdom.

Yes, that is what I desire. As you have been rejoicing in some of the events in your life, I have been rejoicing that so many of My people are ready for partnering with Me in the work I am about to do. Yes, there is a war where I need you to be warriors. But there are also times of refreshment as My princes and princesses. You are called to both roles. Keep listening and watching. Pray at the opportune times in the opportune ways. Know when to fight, and also to be gentle and caring. Look to Me.

Lord, I need another dose of Your grace.

Getting weighed down with all the problems of the world?

It seems that way.

You know what to do with them all, don't you?

Yes, I need to dump them at Your feet.

What is stopping you?

OK, Lord, they are all Yours. I had no way of solving any of them anyway.

And if you did, how would you handle that?

Probably just as badly as I was trying to carry them.

When I bring a problem you can solve, I also give you the grace to do so. Look for the grace before you start to worry.

Lord, how is it that with such gentleness You can change my attitude and take away my burdens? I do feel lighter now.

Isn't it good that it no longer takes several days for you to come to Me before you give me your problems?

It sure is. Thank You so much. Help me not take on any more that doesn't belong to me.

I am with you. I can carry them all. Enjoy My gentle love.

Dear Jesus, for some reason, I am a mess this morning. I need You to take over.

I can do that. Martha is fighting Mary again. The focus has shifted to what needs to be done. You can bring it back to love, joy, and peace. It is not that what you are doing is wrong, but the attitude of having to do them. When things become a burden, rather than a joy, it is a sign that you are taking back the controls. Let go and sink into My embrace. I am ready to take back the controls.

I can do that. Thank You for the gentleness with which You show me that I need correction.

Lord, I finally heard You calling me to prayer ever so gently this morning. Thank You. It is only a half-hour before the alarm would have rung, but You allow me to feel like I am gladly obeying You. And I am.

How does it feel?

Pretty good.

As it should. Today, you will have other chances to obey. Remember that it is good. Not burdensome. Keep dwelling on My love, joy, and peace. It is good to also remember My gentleness. Just as you felt that this morning, so you will see it in new ways through the day. My gentleness also comes through in the way you relate to others, especially the older folks you deal with. I have taught you well. Keep it up.

Perhaps this would be a good day to call the sick and shut-in list this afternoon. Those who answer do appreciate it. And get ready to cook this week. See, I have good works for you to walk in. And none of them will be stressful. Stay in peace. Enjoy My companionship. I am with you at all times. Come follow Me. I am indeed leading you.

And I thoroughly appreciate it. Thank You that I am more often aware of You during the day. It is easier to know You are with me at night, but now it is getting better in the daytime as well. I know this is Your gentle grace.

This is union. Are you satisfied?

Lord, You just made me smile. Yes, I am. At least for the moment. I do not promise I can stay this way. But I am exceedingly grateful.

I can work with that.

Lord, I know You have even more concerns than I know about, so here I am to thank You for Your care and concern for us all. You are in control, and daily we pray that Your kingdom should come, and Your will should be done on earth as it is in heaven. Lord, I do pray that. I also pray for all our deceased loved ones, especially for my husband, Rae, who would have been 80 years old today. Thank You that I get to go to the cemetery where he is buried. Hold him close, Lord, and let him know I still miss him after 28 years.

I do hold him close, and also know all your concerns. My love for you is infinite. So is My love for each of them. But remember that it is not only love, but peace, and joy, and all the other fruits that I have for you and them.

Fear not. Worry not. Let Me take care of all. Just as you have been there for your friends, I am there for them as well as for you. The world may be going through a great shaking, but you are in My hands and I will not stop holding you. Trust Me with everything.

I have been taking good care of you and have no plans to stop. As you care for others, you are caring for Me as well. I also love your gentle touch. I love your ministry of presence. In turn, I give you My Presence. Rest in it. You will be cleansed and refreshed and re-filled. As you hold on to Me, and I hold on to you, it is a wonderful embrace. Allow yourself to feel it. It is good.

Thank You, Lord.

Over the past 50 years or so, You have worked continuously in my life, and I have rededicated my life to You so many times. I have told the story often, and even wrote it in my book. You taught me gently. Just as I asked You to do so. But You have proven to me that following You is the Way, the Truth, and the Life. I am ever so grateful. Yet, I still desire more. And You have assured me that there is a lot more.

Yes, there is. And that will also come gently. Be patient. Do not run ahead of Me or lag behind. I know exactly what you need and desire. Your heart is both rearing to go, and reluctant at the same time. Like a race horse at the start of a race. But you have been well-trained, and will not let the reluctance hold you back. I know how to guide you. It is good.

I remember what it was like before I turned to You. I usually go back as far as when I tried to speak to You, that if You are real, show me, but do it gently. But perhaps I need to go back even further. By the time I asked You that, You were already preparing me to come back to You. Perhaps I need to go back to when I left the Church in arrogance and rebellion. I thought I knew better than the Church, and disagreed with its teaching, and left in the middle of Mass, and did not come back until several years later. I did feel self-righteous, and almost proud of myself for rebelling against what I thought was wrong. But You did bring me back, and You did do it gently. I do thank You.

Do you also remember when you longed to believe, but were not quite there yet?

I do. But it is a bit fuzzy by now. But You worked it all out.

Are you not in a similar situation now with believing that I will bring revival and reformation to the world?

I suppose I am. I want to believe, but right now it is only a hope. I am expecting some major happening, but it seems You are working much more gently than I would want. Yet, once I did accept that You were real, I also did not like how slowly You moved in my life. I kept trying to run ahead of You instead of following You. Now that I am old, running is not an option. But waiting on You, and just following is still a challenge.

So, it is. But by now, you are up to that challenge. Your trust has grown and your desire for union with Me is anchoring you to wherever I want you to be. It is good.

And now I feel Your Presence. Thank You.

Lord, it seems like I am on a spiritual roller-coaster. One day up, then down, then somewhere in between, not knowing what comes next.

Roller coasters used to be fun, but not anymore.

I suppose I have outgrown them.

As it should be. There is a time for everything. Right now, you are in a transition period. You have to wait for the next step. Waiting is often difficult. But small delights can be found even while waiting. Look for them today. Enjoy the scenery until the train moves again.

Remember that trip to Indiana so many years ago. It was a dreary day with occasional misty rain, and your husband was driving through some mountainous area. But you noticed some gentle beauty that every crevice in the hills, seemed to have a little cloud dancing there. You found beauty in a gray and seemingly desolate trip. This is the day the Lord has made. Rejoice and be glad in it.

Thank You, Lord. It sounds a lot better already.

Chapter 9

Faithfulness

Dear Jesus, today I am again asking for You to speak – as Your servant is listening.

Maggie, I never stopped speaking to you. You did grasp parts of what I have been telling you. You feel My love and care. You continue to come to Me even when you think things are not working well in your prayer life. But I see a much larger picture than you do.

I value the small considerate care you provide. You see that I provide you with opportunities to serve Me. But it is not the same as it was when you were younger and healthier.

You worry that I am not pleased or satisfied with you. I have told you many times not to "grade" your prayer time. Yet it is difficult for you to abstain from that. Now you can see that you indeed spent quality time with Me, and that you have 'heard' Me. It is much different than it was, but your faithfulness has matured.

Before – when prayer was difficult, you stayed away, sometimes for months. Now you keep coming daily and even attempt ways of prayer you do not particularly like. I see all that. Yes, there can still be improvements, but it is good.

Dear Jesus, thank You for the prayer meeting yesterday. You assured us that You are using us and plan to use us more. We are to wait and listen to take the opportunities You will give us to bring others to You. It seems all four of us have had the same frustrations that we felt that we were getting distant from You and we were all desperate to hear Your voice again. And we did. Thank You.

Each of you have been hearing My voice, but it has come to you in different ways than you were familiar with for so many years. As you continue to seek Me, you will see it all come together. You have been listening to My prophets in ways you did not have when you first came to Me. Back then you searched the Scriptures and listened to each other as I spoke to you in a more private setting. You hear and see what I am doing on a much larger scale. Your prayers are no longer mostly about your own lives but may also encompass the whole world. It may not seem like progress to you, but it is pleasing to your God.

Lord, is this the maturing process we want to see in our children as well?

Yes. You want them to be less self-centered. Do you see that I am teaching you to also be less self-centered? It does not mean that I care less for your individual issues, but your focus is expanding without losing the intimacy with Me that you still desire.

I still desire the intimacy as well. You continue to need to come to Me and rely on Me – actually even more – as your ministry expands. Yes, it is expanding. I am using you in new ways. Begin to rejoice in it. And your eyes and ears will open to see and hear what I am doing.

You are Mine. I AM your God. You have not left Me, and I will never leave you. My peace will overtake the turmoil you have been feeling. Do come and feel my arms holding you close. I have not changed, but I am answering your prayers to change you to a more mature stage in your life.

The good news is that you can still come to Me as a little child. I welcome the child in you as well as I love the mature servant and friend that child has turned into. Be at peace.

None of the teaching you have received is wasted. You will need all the resources I have given you as you bring along the new

generation I am bringing up in the coming times. Your experiences will be very helpful to them.

Lord, I am remembering when I started working at Joseph House. I was delighted to be serving You in new and exciting and seemingly more important ways, but felt I needed a lot more support and instruction than was available.

That is why your prayer time with Me is so important. You need to discuss with Me what you experience. It is good to discuss it with others as well. I have given you to each other so you can encourage one another – but I must be the focus of all that is going on in your life – particularly as well as in the ministry to which I am calling you.

Lord, I feel Your Presence. It all seems so much more possible now. You have given me a new confidence that I can still be useful to You. But I am also aware of how I will need so much help – continually. Thank You that You do provide it all.

Lord, I need to talk to You about spiritual warfare. When and how are we to use taking authority, warring angels, the power You have given us, the armor we have been given, and probably much more. I do see the necessity of it all but am confused as to what part I have in it all. I do want to be a warrior in Your army, but at 75, and mostly blind and lame, where do I fit in?

I do pray, but I don't see that I am much of a prayer warrior, either. I am not an apostle, though I honor evangelization, I don't see myself as much of an evangelist. I am not a pastor – though some do come to me for advice occasionally – I am a teacher, but of math, not much else – and I am certainly not a prophet. Yet I want to serve You in any way I can and appreciate the opportunities I have of doing so. But on days like yesterday – when I did almost nothing, I felt like a useless servant.

Maggie, I have not complained. I have trained you and continue to do so. As you listen, you learn a lot and must rely on Me to use what you have learned. I only did what I saw My Father

doing. I did His Will. A soldier or a warrior does not fight or do things he thinks need to be done, but what he is commanded to do. You need orders. The orders will come as necessary. A good commander knows how best to use his troops. Trust Me that I am a good commander. Right now, patience and intercession are your orders. Keep at it.

Daily you offer your prayers, works, joys, and sufferings. That is intercession. You often agree in intercession with others, even through messages you hear. The Mass, the Bible study, the rosaries, the prayer meeting, the small group on Fridays – all involve intercession. The impatience comes in when you don't see the results. There are results, but you will see them only later. Just like finding out so many years after the action that the good deeds you did decades ago truly were appreciated.

Even at 75, mostly blind and lame, you still do good deeds. Maybe not as often, but you do. I see it all. I see things that you don't even consider that you are actually doing something good. It is because you have had good training. So now you still need to focus on joy. Rejoice in your mission. It is good. Rejoice in My love and pleasure. Rejoice that you are constantly in My care.

Dear Jesus, thank You for using me yesterday. I'm not sure whether I was any help to You at all in what happened, but I felt that I was serving You in the ministry of presence. A friend called me from South Carolina, and I listened to her for 2 ½ hours with an occasional response. I did not say much as she did the talking, but I listened. She has had a very hard life but seems to be somewhat on her feet. Please help her. She needs You but does not know how to reach You or even that You are the answer to all her troubles. But You led me to listen and occasionally to making her laugh, so I think I was able to serve You. Lord, let me add her to the ones I pray for on a regular basis. I used to pray for her regularly, and I don't know why I stopped. Hold her close, Lord. Help her to see good in the people she deals with.

Lord, I pray for her and for my friends with various forms of mental issues. Lord, You understand them even though few others do. Hold them all close and heal their hurting hearts.

Maggie, I did use you last night, but now I need to heal your hurting heart. All the negativity you listened to is not meant to tear you down. I am still in charge. I have sustained this friend through all the trouble. I do take care of all the ones you pray for. It is good for you to place them in My loving hands. I do love each one and sustain them even though they do not understand.

Before you turned to Me, you were also in difficult times. I have brought you out of all those troubles. I healed you, taught you, forgave you, opened your eyes to see where you were wrong, and helped you correct your flaws. You see how I have worked with another friend. She now loves and serves Me well. But it took putting people like you into her life and giving all of you the grace to love her despite all her troubles. Now she focuses on helping others rather than concentrating on how hard her life has been.

Your job is actually what you did last night. Listening and inserting what encouragement you can and a bit of humor when possible. But do not let their negativity become your burden. Bring it all to Me and let Me be the One Who bears these burdens.

Through grace, your life is good. Long ago, you also yearned for someone to listen to you and understand you. I am the One Who does. And I provided you with My servants who also keep you mentally and emotionally healthy. I have trained you for this ministry through a now deceased difficult person. She is at peace now, but you remember how difficult it was for you and your friends to listen to her for what seemed to be hours at a time. Now you can see why.

It is the same with a different aging friend. I trained you with your mother-in-law and with your aunt. When you gently listen to her, you are serving Me. Last night you served me for 2 ½ hours. I know you love serving Me and lament that you don't have as many opportunities to do so. But you see, the opportunities do come. They are simply different. Just remain aware of My

love. Not just for them, but for you. Being a good friend is a great service. Remember the song "What a friend we have in Jesus." As you listen to your hurting friends, you are imitating Me. And I am honored. Yes, you have this power to make your God smile. So, rejoice.

Thank You so much, Lord. I needed You to put this in a better perspective than what I was feeling. I really am delighted to serve You in any way I can.

You are not to worry about any of those I put in your life. Just give all their issues to Me. They do not know how to do it themselves. They need you to do it for them. And I take it all as if they asked. This is your faithfulness as well as Mine.

Lord, that is a tremendous thought. When we intercede for someone, it is as if they themselves were all to come to You for help?

You did not know the power of your intercessions. As you pray, I listen and answer. Whether it is you who does the praying or the person in need of that prayer, the answer is the same – it is for their good. Keep praying for others – but do not let it become a chore or a burden – not a have-to but a want-to. Let Me be in charge even about who and when and how often you pray for others. It has to be voluntary not forced. All the burdens are on Me – I want you free.

Thank You so much, Lord. You know me through and through. You know how easily I can fall into thinking everything is my responsibility. I give You back any controls of my life that I have unknowingly tried to usurp. You are in charge – and I am so glad that I am not. Your faithfulness is awesome.

You are beginning to see that I am working at all you pray about. You may not see the results, but now believe I know how to best run things. You do know Me better and are delighted every time I reveal another aspect of My Being to you. Both your faith and your love for Me are growing.

Lord, I thank You that You take such a personal interest in me and my life. I remember how desperately I wanted someone, anyone, to know and understand me in my teens. Now in my seventies, I know it is You I wanted all my life. I had You right with me but was not aware. So, I kept searching until You finally showed me that You are the only one that can fill that need in my life. And now that I realize that, You allow me to have others in my life who also know and understand me.

You are now seeing the truth in "Seek ye first the Kingdom of God, and His righteousness, and all these things will be added on to you."

To which I can only respond, "Alleluia!"

Thank You that You helped me through my physical issues earlier in the night. All the discomfort seems to be gone, and I expect I will be fine the rest of the day.

Did your mind go blank again?

It did. I seem to be more tired than usual. I need You to pick a topic, as I can't seem to think much right now.

I can do that. There is a struggle inside you about wanting your parish to be more active in defending truth and freedom. You see your priests doing a much better job than what was done before they came to the parish, but they are sticking to the guidelines given them by the Church. You can't fault them for that but would like to see them in a more active role in fighting the evil you see in government and society. Keep praying for them. Keep loving and supporting them. They are in a very difficult situation having to be obedient to superiors. At this point, you can speak more freely than they can. I will move My own way in their lives and give them the wisdom they need.

Be careful not to tear down or criticize. They get enough of that on a daily basis. Keep praying for their health and well-being. They are under tremendous spiritual attack. Fight for them. I have given you weapons of warfare. Here is an occasion to

use them. They are effective even if no-one else knows you are engaged in this battle. It is a spiritual war, not a physical one. But the enemy gladly inflicts physical stress and pain on My servants. You need to infiltrate the enemy's camp and come against such attacks. I will give you the occasions to do such battle. But you must do it without being noticed. You will be My under-cover warrior. Soon you will be joined by others as well. The clergy really needs such support.

Lord, I accept this commission. Let me do it well.

I will guide you every step of the way. Stay alert.

Thank You, Lord.

Dear Jesus, please help me do all that I need to do.

I am with you. Have you noticed that your activity level has increased? I am providing you with good works to walk in. They seem rather ordinary now, but continue to be faithful in them, and the extraordinary will emerge in time. I am working in your life as well as in your world. You are beginning to see what I am doing in your life and ministry.

Yes, you have a ministry. It may seem small now, but as long as you are available to Me, I can grow it and touch more people than you can imagine. It is good that you tend to focus on what is currently before you and not worry too much about what may or may not happen in the future. This is My gift to you. It allows Me to work in and through you without you trying to direct the process. I can prepare you for what is to come without letting you fret about it.

Here again is a case where we tend to misjudge You. You do not withhold Your reasons for doing things from us, but if we knew them, we would worry more than necessary. Our trust in You needs to grow so much more. At least mine does. I have often been upset when something happens that You did not warn me that it was coming. Now I am grateful that You did not. I did not have time to meddle in Your business if I did not know about it. But You give me the opportunity to affect matters through prayer. I suppose that is why praying in the Spirit is so necessary and effective. We don't need to know the details but can agree with You about whatever the topic You choose for us to pray about. Help me to remember to do so more often. It, too, is a ministry.

Indeed, it is. And when someone pops up in your dreams that you had not thought of in a while, that is a clue to pray for them. You may not know how your prayers for him work but be assured that they do.

You have heard and answered so many of our prayers for healing lately, and we thank You, so please keep doing that.

Yes, this is a good time to pray in the Spirit. Keep doing so, and I will take care of this and other situations as they come. Keep trusting Me but keep praying as well. I do use your prayers for good.

Lord, I got everything I needed to do done.

Right now, it is balanced. You do not have to exhaust yourself doing things you dislike, but they can be accomplished a little at a time. Your prayer life is also like that. Other than this time you spend with me during the night, and the Mass, your prayers need not be long and complicated. Nor should they be something you dread or avoid. A loving glance toward Me is very appreciated.

It is a passing touch or a kiss. Spiritual marriage is a continual romance. It is to be enjoyed by both parties. Let go of the dutiful compliance and allow yourself just to love. Dance with Me again. Maybe not physically, but in your mind and heart. Laugh with Me. Cry with Me. The key words are "with Me." I am with you all the time. That means you are with Me all the time as well. Let it be a delight for both of us.

Dear Jesus, thank You for waking me and giving me the strength to come to You. I had a hard time getting to sleep last night. I finally got comfortable enough to have some deep sleep and did not want to get up. But You can give me more rest in a few minutes than I could get in several hours, so I refused to be robbed of Your company this morning. I remembered what You told me about the romance. I want to participate in that romance, and here I am.

Maggie, it is good that you chose to come to Me. Sometimes the body does not cooperate with the spirit. But I have overcome all that. I receive your love and shower Mine upon you. You have a book in your bookcase that you wanted to read for many years but never did. It would be worth the effort to try to read it now. No, not now in the middle of the night, but in the next few days. I want to show you more of My love, in such a way that it becomes the driving force of your life. This is the union with Me that you long for. It is the union with you that I long for. See if you can find it and make the effort to read it. Then let's talk about it.

Lord, this is how spiritual direction worked when I got started.

Yes, I am your ultimate Spiritual Director. But I am willing to share the office with your priests. But I am more easily available right now. And you need a more personal touch than you can receive from anyone else. I can hold you close. I can touch you in the middle of the night. I am with you all the time. See, the invisibility has its advantages.

Lord, You made me smile again. I have complained to You about Your invisibility for years. I am finally beginning to appreciate it. But I don't promise to stop complaining altogether.

I am counting on that. It makes Me smile when you do.

Lord, today should be a calm day, and there are small jobs that need to be done. Please help me not waste my time. I have not even begun to find the book You mentioned last night but will try today. Lord, when You tell me things and I don't do them, I feel like I have failed in faithfulness. It seems like such an insignificant thing to not look for a book, but when I thought about it, it did not seem to be a good time to do so. Then I simply forgot the rest of the day.

You are still trying to legalize your relationship with Me. Not everything is a command to be immediately obeyed. Who benefits from your forgetting to do something? Or your feeling bad about it? With your friends, if you forget something, you just quickly apologize.

When I did a miracle, and told people not to tell anyone, they did not follow My directions. Did I get angry or take back their healing? No.

You are right, Lord. We so misjudge You. We are expecting wrath at every turn. We forget Your kindness and gentleness.

Lord, Your love is amazing! I walked to the bookcase, and the very first book I looked at was the one You want me to read. I now have it out and will begin reading with my little machine.

Lord, thank You for allowing me to do a kindness for someone. It feels really good.

It is good to be kind. It is also good that you made the effort to read a chapter in the book. It is also good that peace has returned to your heart. I do not want you to be in turmoil. Learn from Me.

Even under much opposition, I remained calm. I was able to get frustrated with the lack of faith of My friends, and get angry at the desecration of the Temple, but I stayed at peace within Me. I give you this peace. I kept in contact with My Father in prayer in order to maintain this peace. You must keep in contact with Me or any Person of the Trinity to keep from depleting the peace I give you.

I suppose it is that we are leaky vessels and need to be refilled often.

Sort of. But you can also think of it as consuming the fuel in order to keep going. Like gas in a car, or food for your body. What you put in is sufficient for a while but needs to be refilled as it is used up. Prayer is the refueling. So is Mass, and the Rosary, and good works, and adoration. Think of these things as the food for the soul and spirit.

You do not eat only one kind of food. Some are more nourishing than others, and some taste better than others, but together they keep you going. Listening to the messages of My servants is also good food. For you, reading may be difficult, but like a dish that takes time and effort to make, it will be worth it. For others, reading is easier, but something else may require more effort. The effort is your faithfulness.

I appreciate whatever effort you put into prayer. Not because I need your prayer, but more like how you appreciate when your students work at learning math. It edifies you to see them doing well. You enjoy their success. I enjoy your success and well-being. My love for you is returned to Me fulfilled. Like in Isaiah 55. As the rain and snow do not return to Me void, but do their job, so My gifts to you do the same. And your gifts to others also do the same. I made you in My image. I made you to enjoy the success of those you love just as I do. This is also union. It is very good.

Lord, I listened to some messages yesterday that make me grateful for being part of several parts of Your Church. Whether or not the denominations ever unite, they are united within me, and within those of us who value all the aspects we now see. You have a way of doing what You promised in a way that people do not expect.

Is this one of those things? When You were on the earth, people expected Your Kingdom to be different than it is. Perhaps Your uniting Your Ecclesia is not the denominations coming together and becoming one. But it is those of us You have been teaching, agreeing with one another despite our different denominations.

We don't need to be alive to be unified. We can be united to the faith of our predecessors and Saints. I can appreciate and follow my Catholic faith and still learn from and appreciate the way You are working in the lives of those I listen to. Those who would not be comfortable in a Catholic church but have a sincere love for You. They hear from You, and have devoted their lives to You, and powerfully do Your Will. What a joy to be able to get the benefit of all. This is what Fr. Bertalucci kept saying many years ago. "None of us have it all together, but together we have it all."

And just like My disciples, you feel a bit outside the norm. They were still Jews, but different. You are still Catholics, or as in the case of some of your prayer partners, Protestants, but totally united in loving and listening and obeying Me. I do not ask you to leave your traditions behind but am enlarging your vision and focus. I need people who can be flexible enough to accept and perhaps minister to people who are quite different from those they usually see. I have introduced you to people you would not have even considered worth speaking to, and you now see how I am working with and through them.

I did the same on earth. I was criticized for eating with tax collectors and sinners. Welcome to My world. You will also be criticized. But as long as you follow Me, it will all be worthwhile. I am in it all with you.

Lord, I think I am in the center of Your Will in this. When I took care of my mother, I felt I was finally doing Your Will. Now I am not doing much at all but feel like I am thinking more in line with You.

Trust these feelings. And allow yourself to rejoice in them. You have often longed to be set apart for Me. This is how you are becoming ready to do My Will. The song you sing, "purify my heart" is happening. I am purifying your heart so that you can be set apart for Me and be ready to do My Will.

Lord, how is it that you touch me so deeply with songs when I am the most unmusical person I know? You have done this before, too. No, I am not complaining, just amused. Thank You.

Dear Jesus, thank You for a day of rest. I thought the chapters of my new book can be based on the fruits of the Spirit. I think I am ready to work on this.

I see that you are. And I will be right here with you to help and continue to inspire you. This is a desire of My heart. I long to reveal Myself to My people. As the harvest comes, there will be a need for practical teaching. Sort-of like tutoring. I have prepared you for this.

Lord, that is an awesome thought. My tutoring being elevated.

You will need a closer collaboration with My Spirit. Yes, the Holy Spirit. He will explain things to you, and, in turn, you will explain things in writing. There will be times when the words will come quickly, and at other times you will need to ask Him for help. It will be and already is an exciting time.

Lord, I am feeling once again like I am doing Your Will. What a joy to know You are guiding me and that this is something You want. Yet, before I get too full of myself, perhaps this is Your way to keep me busy. Either way, I thank You. You know I cannot do a lot of things I might want to do, so You give me something I can do despite my age and impairments. Thank You.

How many times I have told you that My love for you is greater than you can imagine. It is.

Thank You, Lord.

Lord, last night when I went to bed, You showed me that my new way of intercession gives me satisfaction. For once I did not doubt that I prayed enough. I knew You listened to me, and I felt

Your approval. So often I feel my prayers are so feeble and inadequate. But You have never complained. Thank You.

This is why I keep telling you not to grade your prayers. I see things much differently than you can. Sometimes just a look is an acceptable prayer. It is not measured as enough or not enough. It is relationship. You are Mine, and I am yours. It does not change. I do not love you more or less according to the amount or quality of your prayers. I simply love you. All of you. You are not yet perfect. That is part of My Father's plan. It gives the Trinity a project to work on.

You just made me smile again.

I see. Me, too. It is not that you are a project, but perfecting your faithfulness is the project. You like having a project. So does your God. It is another way you are made in the image and likeness. But back to satisfaction. You once said you would not be satisfied until you have total union with Me. I took that as a challenge. Last night you felt a bit of that satisfaction.

There is much more ahead. As your first book is published, there will be a certain satisfaction with that. Whether it sells well or not, there was a lot of work involved in it, and it is good. Right now, you are not quite sure how to go about with the next one. But the guidance will come, and it will also be good, because it is a joint project. A part of that union.

But it cannot be all-consuming. There are other parts of your life that need attention as well. Do not grade every action or inaction. I am the judge. You are not. Be patient. The first book was not done in one year. This one will also take some time. Not as many as the first but let Me be in charge of the timing.

I see that You need to be in control and not me. Why is that so hard for us humans to comprehend?

It is that fallen nature. But I have overcome it and am teaching you to overcome as well. Trust Me that I can do it.

There is that smile again. Thank You. Keep working on me. I really do appreciate it.

Lord, I heard a message that confirmed something You showed me recently. It said that the reason we need to pray is not because we should, or because You demand it, but because You have chosen to include us in whatever You desire to do. That You desire our partnership with You.

I get a picture of a little kid helping to bake cookies. They would not be made without the kid helping. When they are done, the kid takes credit and is delighted, as is the parent. Eventually, the kid is able to make the cookies when asked to do so.

You are like the parent who patiently teaches us how to do things. We don't even realize how little we actually help but are allowed to feel that our contribution is valuable. In time, as we learn, it does become valuable.

You rely on us to do things You have trained us to do. But in all of this, it is the relationship with You that is most important. We rely on You, and soon You begin to rely on us. Often You have to clean up our messes because we try to do things before we are ready. You continue to encourage us and help us learn how to do things better than we thought we could.

Yes, it is something like that and more. There is also the invisibility thing. I choose to remain invisible so my people become the visible part of doing My Will. You are My hands and feet and voice. And at times, you also become invisible as when you engage in intercessory prayer. But you are visible to Me, and I do use your prayers to accomplish much good.

Then there is the other invisible army of angels that take direction from those who pray. They await your commands. I am teaching you to have much greater effect than you can see. I waste nothing. All the teaching you have had is coming into use. I have trained you to be a warrior. Someday you will see the results which are now invisible to you. But for now, keep praying and interceding and be ready for My use. I will supply all you need, and you will delight in the magnitude of such a partnership.

My love for you is already perfect, but your love for Me will continue to grow. When anything is done out of love, it becomes so much more enjoyable for both parties.

Lord, how come we did not see any of this before?

When you first learn to count, you do not see that it will come in handy when you are in higher level math courses. In first grade, you are not concerned with algebraic equations. But without knowing how to count, you could not do algebra. I have to teach you the basics first, and then you can learn the reason for having to learn them. This is why I keep telling you not to judge even your own progress. I see a much bigger picture. I know the reasons behind every circumstance. Your faithfulness will bear fruit. Trusting Me keeps you in peace. I want that peace for you. It is My gift.

Thank You, Lord. I will use that peace now.

Dear Jesus, I don't understand what is happening in the Church. It seems You are exposing corruption in there just as You are exposing it in the country. It is very sad. I thought we were finally having some relief after the scandals of a few years ago, but apparently, You are once again cleaning house.

It has to be done once in a while. But your job is to pray, not worry. You must leave this matter in My hands and let me deal with all the parties involved. I see a much bigger picture than you can. Remember that I can bring good out of the worst disasters. Keep praying for all those involved. But do not allow this, or any other matter to steal your peace or joy.

Lord, you are so right. I have been letting it get to me. It is Your business, not mine.

No, I do not want you to just forget about it. I allowed you to be concerned because I want you to pray and intercede for all those involved. I have given you weapons of warfare. You are a part of My army. This is neither a time to rush ahead of your duty, nor a time to abandon it altogether. I require your faithfulness. There is corruption in the nation, and there is corruption in the Church. I am revealing both so My people can use their weapons to fight the evil that is trying to destroy both the nation and the

Church. Increase the intensity of your prayers, not the intensity of your feelings.

Pray in the Spirit whenever you feel upset or angry or sad about these situations. Your feelings do not help the situation, but your prayers do. I send forth My angels and righteousness as you pray. I await your prayers as I choose to partner with My Bride, the holy Church, to do My Will. You are a part of My Body. I choose to use you in this and many other matters. But you are not to get upset, but rather to seek My Will, and follow My leading.

Beyond that, focus on the good that there still is in the Church. Be grateful for all that is good and right and holy. Fight the evil but be grateful for the good. Do not condemn. Do not seek revenge. Do not ask for My wrath to come upon anyone. Leave it all to Me but keep praying.

Thank You, Lord. These are clear directions. Help me to follow them well. And I do thank You for all the good that the Church does, as well as for allowing me to have a part in that.

Now your peace and joy are coming back as you focus on what good you can do and are doing. My love for you continues. Your love for Me is growing. It is good.

After several things needed fixing in the house, I was surprised that I was not worried or upset about them.

Maggie, it is good that such things no longer bother you. You are right, I have had to work hard to get you to this point. Peace is a gift, but not everyone receives it easily. And it is also a fragile gift. It can be quickly broken or lost. But it can also be nurtured and it can grow. Sort-of like a potted plant. It needs the right amount of water and sunlight, and good soil, and even the right size container. But my Father is a good gardener. He knows and provides all you need.

Lord, I just realized that so many things in life are like that. But I now see it from the perspective of the faithful gardener. He does all the work, and what does He get out of it?

He gets the pleasure of seeing it grow and blossom and become all it was meant to be. This is what He wants for all His creation.

So, that is another way to please God. Just being what He created and tended and cared for?

Pretty much. But He also gave you more gifts than He gave to plants. You do have some responsibilities that plants do not have. You have intellect and will. They can also be used to please your God, but they can also cause problems.

I suppose we are back to submission and surrender. When we are convinced of Your goodness and love and care, and that You know better than we do, it is easier to submit to that. This is why You delight in revealing Yourself to us. But how easily we miss that.

You have an enemy that wants to convince you that I am not good and loving and caring. When you believe that lie, things can go terribly wrong. This is why I delight in revealing Myself to you. The Truth does set you free. Free to submit and surrender because the One to whom you submit and surrender is all-good, all-loving, all-knowing, all-caring.

My response to that is awe and wonder, and gratitude, and also love. I used to think that loving You was so difficult, but once I understood Who You really are, loving You is so natural. Thank You.

At the beginning of each Lent, I often have elaborate plans similar to New Year's resolutions, and then abandon them just as quickly. Then I feel I have failed in my devotion to the Lord. This time, I again had thoughts that I should start more projects and I was inspired to ask Him before I committed myself.

If this is not what You want, I am open to other ideas. But I will need lots of help.

You are already involved in several projects. It would get too difficult. Do not make Lent into a stressful time. I finally have you concentrating on My love, joy, and peace. Lenten practices are not to crowd these out of your life but bring them in and

grow them. As long as it is a "get-to "rather than a "have-to" then it is good. Otherwise, it is counterproductive. You do not have to impress Me or anyone else about your commitment. I already know and love you. So do all who are supposed to know and love you.

So, it is not what I do, but why I do it. And I see that I was trying to impress You. Humility does not come easy for me. But, of course, You are right. If I do these extra things, I will only do them to check off the list of 'specially for Lent,' not because I think they will make me wiser. Suddenly the temptation of Eve comes to mind. Forgive Me, Lord, for trying to show off.

Isn't it good that you now come to Me with your plans before you jump into them? Before you started talking with Me on a daily basis, you would have gone through much turmoil trying to keep up with such a plan. That is not My Will for you. I want My peace, joy, and love to be central in your life. Let Me lead the training. See, you were about to take the controls of your life back. But this time, you consulted Me before you did it. And now you don't have to go through that process again. Trust Me that I will teach you all that you need to know.

Lord, I thank You. I do trust You, and I do want You at the controls of my life. I am beginning to see that the thoughts, words, and deeds are secondary to the motives and attitudes. Good thoughts, words, and deeds can be contaminated by the wrong motives and attitudes. Thank You for keeping me from diving off another cliff.

When I want you to take up cliff-diving, I will certainly let you know and provide the power to do it. But not now.

That is reassuring.

I'm glad to help. Now go and sleep with that smile on your face and know that I am also smiling.

Sometimes You make it so easy to obey.

Having trouble praying?
I sure am.

Let Me help.

I think You already are helping. I feel Your Presence.

Yes, you do. I am here. Let Me simply love you tonight. Not for any other reason than that I love you. Yes, I do appreciate your efforts to do more especially for Lent, but you still have trouble comprehending unconditional love. Stop trying to comprehend it, and just accept and enjoy it. Don't think too much. It is not a matter of the mind. Peter was also overcome at the Transfiguration.

Is it that I see You differently now, that I seem to be speechless when I try to come to You? Am I more aware of Your Divinity that I have trouble remembering Your humanity?

Not exactly. It is more of a loss of control. You no longer come to Me with an agenda. You do not know what I want to talk to you about, and you are out of ideas. You cannot be in control.

Actually, that is an answer to prayer, isn't it? I want You to be in control. But I don't seem to handle it well.

That is why I have told you many times not to "grade" your prayers. There are times when it is not instruction you need. At least not the kind of instruction you are used to. There are some things that bypass the mind. As an educator, that is a more difficult concept for you.

Is it that You are trying to give my mind a rest?

No, not really. It is not something to understand. It is simply to be experienced.

OK, Lord, I will stop analyzing it. As long as You don't mind my coming to You and becoming speechless, I suppose I shouldn't mind it either.

But keep on coming anyway. It will bear good fruit.

Dear Jesus, thank You for a calm and quiet day yesterday. Thank You also that my eating was under control, and I even got a nap once again in the afternoon. Then You played with me and the time this night. When I went to bed a little after 9, I playfully asked you if it would be possible to sleep for about three hours before I had to wake up. I did fall asleep easily, and when I did wake up from very deep sleep, I looked at my clock and saw 1:01. I smiled and thanked You, as I had not expected You to grant that request. I went back to sleep, slept deeply again, and woke up thinking it might be at least 3 AM, looked at the clock, and it said 12:36. Then I really thanked You. Either You were playing with me, or my blindness was the cause of misreading the clock the first time, I really appreciated it all. So now it is a bit after 3:00, and I don't have to get up until 8:00. You have blessed me with more sleep than I usually get.

Let's stick with the playing with you story. I get to play once in a while, too. You watched a lot of news yesterday and it was all so serious and negative. Both you and I needed a bit of levity. Yes, the world is in trouble in many ways, but I am working and My grace abounds. Do not fear about world events. Know that I will continue to hold you close and answer even your playful requests. Right now, you feel My presence and peace. Soak it in and spread it as you go about this day. Peace on earth begins in the hearts of My people. And I am gathering many more people and letting them become Mine.

The revival will not be stopped. It will erupt in many places. It may not be on the news yet, but it will be. Asbury is just the beginning. Trust Me that I can keep it going. When you first came to Me, it took a long time before your faith was strong enough to withstand the assaults of the enemy. But I gave you all the help you needed. I am now doing the same with many others.

Lord, trust is not a fruit of the Spirit, is it? But faithfulness requires or at least engenders trust. Because You are faithful, we can trust You. As we become faithful, You can trust us.

Yes, that is a good way to look at it. And peace is very much connected with trust and faithfulness.

Lord, during this Lent, I think You are preparing for us a spiritual fruit salad. This concept makes me laugh. You are awesome!

See, even if you fast, I will not let you starve. It is good to laugh. Loving relationships need to be enjoyable. Enjoy My love.

Thank You so much, Lord.

After a hospital stay, I had a new schedule for taking medicine which I thought would also correspond well with my prayer times at night. But then when I could not sleep during the night, I questioned whether the Lord was calling me to prayer before the time I thought would work well with my medicine.

I was not sure whether You were calling me to pray after affirming the new schedule yesterday.

New schedule or not, you can come to Me at any time. I will welcome you. Do not legalize time with Me. Prayer is to be loving relationship, not a regimen. You have been wondering if I stopped teaching you because I have seen and responded to your physical needs. The times of prayer have become shorter because I love you, not because I have nothing to teach you. And now you are falling asleep. It is all right to go back to bed. I do not go away. I am with you always. Be at peace.

Thank You, Lord.

The next night, I was full of thanksgiving, as my strength was returning after the hospital stay.

It seems I have entered Your gates with thanksgiving. Now perhaps I could enter Your courts with praise. You are the source of all the goodness and love and care that I have so lavishly been endowed with. It is not that I earned or merited it in any way, but just because You are Love, and Goodness, and Peace, and Joy, and all the other fruits of the Spirit. You are all those things, and having made us in Your image and likeness, You want us to bear such fruit as well.

Thank You for scolding me yesterday about legalizing prayer. Of course, You were right. I had fallen back into looking at prayer as a "should" rather than a loving embrace. Lord, I apologize.

Apology accepted. It is easy to slip back into old ways of thinking. For how many years did you consider prayer a "Should?" Now that you have been faithful to it for a longer stretch of time, it is easy to forget that it is to be a joy and a pleasure instead. Not only is the action important, but the attitude behind it. This applies to many other things in your life as well.

After missing Mass for five days, you were delighted to be able to get up and get ready and have enough strength to do it again. It is that delight that I look for and am pleased with. Happiness and joy may not be the same, but they are similar. I want you happy and full of joy. That is the abundant life. Not material wealth or other things people consider important, but the relationship you have with Me. You don't have to understand it, just enjoy it.

Lord, I don't understand it, but am infinitely grateful for it, and do enjoy it.

That's My girl.

Dear Jesus, thank You for the time of prayer and fellowship my friend and I had yesterday. We did pray for the nation, and You did join us Lord, I thank You that You not only hear our prayers but are delighted to guide us in prayer so we can partner with You in doing the Father's Will. It is not that You need us, it is that You choose to have us participate in all You do. What an honor!

You see that I do not consider anyone insignificant. Regardless of any limitations, I can accomplish great things through the prayers and fellowship of even a very few of My friends. There were only two of you there, but I have a whole cloud of witnesses that joined you. You felt My power and can be assured that your prayers make a difference. You will see some results, but others will take a while.

Lord, how different prayer has become in our lives. It is no longer a "have to" but a privilege to unite with You and Your cloud of witnesses. There is still a part that is a "need to," but somehow it is different.

Yes, it is different. Have you noticed that your prayers are generally unselfish. They are "other-focused" rather than self-absorbed. Your circle of influence has expanded. Yes, you still care deeply about family and friends, but you now see a bigger picture. And the good news is that you make a difference in all the circumstances you bring to Me. Whether they are small or huge, I listen and act. And I have resources you cannot see that I can set in motion to answer your prayers. I have legions of angels at My command. Keep bringing me all your concerns. I will know what to do about them.

My mind is blank again. Is there anything You would like to talk about?

Not right now. But be alert for a topic through the day.

Dear Jesus, thank You for giving me a topic.

The topic is inspired by last week's Bible study. We talked about how Your resurrected body seemed different from Your body before Your death. How people did not recognize You at first, but then realized it was You. I was thinking about all this, and remembered a diagram of what our lives are supposed to be like.

There was a circle with three wavy arrows in it. A bigger one for Spirit at the top, a medium on for Psychologic in the middle and a narrow one for physical on the bottom. This was to represent what our lives were supposed to be like. The Spiritual dominating, the psychological following, and the physical being the least important. But when our sin nature came, we tend to turn it upside down and the physical becomes the primary force, the psychological then follows, and the spiritual can become nullified.

Our world has a lot of people that exhibit this. But You had it right. The spiritual aspect of your life was the dominant force. The others followed in good order.

But after Your resurrection, the physical was altered and was completely at the command of the spiritual. Spiritual laws took over, and physical did not interfere. That is why You could appear and disappear as You desired, and when the time came, ascend into Heaven.

Lord, does this make sense at all? It seems to make sense to me. I had never even thought about all this, but since the topic came up at Bible study, and I needed a topic to talk to You about, I think You inspired all this within me.

Yes, it does make sense. It is not a theological dogma but does illustrate the idea in an understandable way. There is nothing wrong about wondering about or questioning Biblical realities. It says in Philippians to think on the things above. That is what you were doing, and as I have often answered your questions in the past, I cleared this one up. It is good.

Thank You, Lord.

Today, I was able to pay my bills, take a nap, finish my laundry, and work on book two. Then I still had time just to relax. I also listened to two great teachings and was more aware of You during the day. Thank You.

One of those teachings prompted me to thank You for the salvation of all my household. I consider everyone who has ever slept here to be my household, so I started thanking You for the salvation of each one. I may not see the results yet, but Your Word promises that if I believe in You, I shall be saved, and my whole household. So, if You said it, it is done. Whether or not I get to see it, You see the end from the beginning, so I can be assured that it is so.

Then the other teaching was about doing what we were created for. Lord, You have brought me through many phases, and the current phase is to be an author. I was not terribly convinced that it is what I am to be now, but I was assured that it is where I am. I don't have to be famous, just faithful. That is what gave me the push to work more on book 2.

You see, I have been working in your life. It is not the number of minutes that you spend in prayer that is important, but that you are alert to My desires for you. You used to be delighted that I gave you the gift of service. You knew you were happiest when serving Me and others. But as your body has aged, you are not able to serve in the same way. But your secondary gift of encourager is coming to maturity. Your books are to encourage others to a closer walk with Me. It is your calling right now. It does not have immediate rewards built in. You do not see the effects of your work as easily. But I see them, and I am pleased. It is good.

One day after praying for several of my friends who were troubled, the Lord answered:

It is good to bring such matters to Me. It is also good to continue to pray. But you are not to worry. You have put each situation in My hands, and I will take care of them. Your part of the job is now to give thanks. Notice that I have allowed people to come to you to request prayer. You served Me by being available to listen and to join with others to lift these matters up to Me.

This is a ministry. It may not look like much of a ministry, but you just listened to a message about being faithful in small things. I have trained your heart to go out to other people's needs. It is so you can bring them to My heart, as My heart works the same way. This is the third of your three s's. You have been practicing the first two, submission and surrender. Now the supplication is in full force. But once you have brought such matters before Me, it is time for thanksgiving. You do not have to plead, or beg, or nag Me, as I have heard you the first time. I am faithful to answer. It is in the thanksgiving that you persist in prayer. The faith and trust that is so pleasing to the Father, is solidified through thanksgiving. As in your first book, I supply the grace, and you supply the gratitude. It is a good partnership.

Lord, I do thank You. Thank You for hearing and answering each of my prayers. Thank You that others have also agreed in prayer for all these requests. Thank You for allowing me to be a part of so many people's lives. And most of all, I thank You that You do hear and answer these prayers. Thank You for however You choose to answer them, and whatever timeline You have for the solutions to all these problems. They are now Your problems, and I know You will take care of them in much better ways than I would even imagine. Thank You for this ministry. Thank You also for such clear instruction. You have not only heard my prayers, but You have satisfied my longing for hearing clearly from You. Thank You for that as well.

Dear Jesus, thank You again for yesterday's teaching. Several times during the day, I was able to simply thank You for having heard my prayers and for whatever Your answer will be.

Come, Holy Spirit, I need help as my mind went blank.

Yesterday you learned a new part to intercession. Rather than teaching you something else now, I want you to continue to practice what you have learned. So many times, I have taught you things and you were delighted with the teaching, but quickly forgot it. That is like the birds eating the seeds on the path. This one has to be planted deep inside you, so it can form deep and strong roots and produce good fruit. I prepared the soil of your heart by giving you very few teachings lately. I had to make you thirsty for My voice. I plowed the soil during that drought. Now the seed has been sown, and the rain of practice will fall on that the seed will have a chance to sprout. Thanksgiving leads to praise. Praise leads to My arms. As you practice, feel My arms enfold you and rejoice. I am with you, and you are doing My will.

Thank You so much, Lord.

Dear Jesus, we had another disappointing election day this week, and yet we still hope things will get better. The country is at a point where only You can sort it out. There is much evil, incompetence, and apathy. We need Your Kingdom to come and Your Will to be done, but we seem to see the opposite. We are told by the prophets that You are indeed moving the angel armies of heaven to shake the earth back into what You desire. We do get glimpses of Your actions, but we are back to that invisibility thing that has so often frustrated me. But I will trust You and believe You are indeed doing much behind the scenes.

In my own life, You have worked wonders. I am much calmer and relying on You rather than myself. Even my health is starting to improve, and I don't hurt as much these days. Thank You for that. You have managed to use me in other people's lives despite my feebleness and uncertainties. I also thank You for that. My love for You has grown, and I know Your love for me is much greater than I can even imagine. You are also working wonders in the lives of those I love.

I am working behind the scenes in national and world affairs. Do not get discouraged. You see what I can do on a smaller scale in your own life and the lives of those around you. Multiply that by the number of those who hear My voice and pray. It will eventually become visible. Pray for the world, but concentrate on your own world to know what I can accomplish. The final victory is assured, but not every battle is won immediately. Keep fighting the battles you are confronted with. As you win each one, it becomes a part of the greater victory. But also take time to enjoy My love and care and peace and joy. Even in wartime, there are moments of peace and joy if you are aware of them. Stay positive. It will help you get through the difficulties. Rely on Me even more. I will handle all your cares.

Thank You, Lord. It is so good to belong to You.

Chapter 10

Self-control, Modesty, and Chastity

I left self-control for the last chapter, not just because it is the last one mentioned in Galatians 5, but because I have had so much trouble acquiring it over the years. I tend to overdo things. And sometimes underdo things. Most of my adult life I have been overweight, under-exercised, a barely passable housekeeper, jumping into things before thinking or asking for directions, etc. But the Lord is good, and exceedingly patient, and now in my later years has given me grace to improve.

Dear Jesus, I heard recently that denying oneself is essential for following You. I have failed in this. I considered I have enough pains and frustrations from my physical problems that I need not deny myself any further. I now see that this is a deception. As I say the preparatory prayer, and offer myself completely to You, there is no living sacrifice but just endurance. No wonder I have felt I was not hearing You well. There is still a lot of self-indulgence in my life – my eating, my likes and dislikes, comfort, and at times – often – insisting on my own ways.

So, what will you do about these things?

I don't know. I suppose listening to You is essential. Any plan I might come up with is likely to fail. I either try to do things too fast or too elaborately and soon give up. Only Your ways can work. But I am afraid I will miss Your plan.

Are you willing to wait for My plan?

I think I have to.

Yes, but are you willing? Even waiting is an act of your will.

OK, Lord, I choose to be willing to wait for Your direction, however You choose to give it to me.

See, that is a first step to surrendering to Me. No instant holiness. This will take time and effort.

What about fasting?

Fasting is good – what would you like to fast from?

I have several options.

This again is an act of the will.

Here again I need clear direction as I have failed in this so often.

Wait again. I will give you the direction – trust Me that you will be able to recognize and obey it.

OK, Lord, I trust in You.

Lord, I have heard an evangelist is having tent meetings, and many people are giving their lives to You. Please make it stick. Let their lives be truly transformed. I remember when I first came to You, I felt like I had to do it over and over again before I felt it was real. But You continued to accept my feeble attempts and did come into my life – and transformed it. Thank You. Please continue to bless these meetings and protect this servant of Yours, and all who help him. Raise up many great evangelists and let this renewal sweep the world. We certainly need it.

Fr. Garrity wrote on one of my papers years ago that the greatest claim we have on You is our need. Your world needs You.

I know how great the need is. I am meeting it. Much great evil is exposed – but the greater good grows silently. When a tree falls, it is quick and loud. But when one grows, it is slow and silent. Yet there are many trees growing, and blooming, and even bearing fruit – silently, slowly, but relentlessly. This is My way of working. Yes, there are signs and wonders, but the growth and transformation are not as easy to see at first. I am still working on you after 48 years. But you know without a doubt that I love

you and will never abandon you. What I have and am doing for you, I can and will do for many others. Keep praying. Even when you have to force yourself to pray, it is effective. This is a part of denying yourself. Did I not tell you that the direction on how to deny yourself will come and you will not miss it? When you exercised on the bike and prayed a Rosary, you did not want to, but you still did it. When you were tired of typing, you finished the job regardless of how you felt. None of this was spectacular – but I see and am pleased. All you saw was that the attitude was not quite right. But I saw obedience, commitment, and love in what you did most of the day.

Lord, I thank You. Even when I think I am failing You bring good out of it.

You see that My ways and thoughts are better?

I do indeed.

Good. Now learn from Me and do the same for others. This is like the growth of a forest. The seeds fall, and more growth follows. Keep working on being joyful. I will nudge you through the day.

Do you see that you have become much more disciplined than you were a few years ago?

Yes, I do in some areas. But then my physical limitations have required it.

And do I not have the option of allowing those limitations?

Yes, You do, but I don't believe You cause them. I don't think You want me in pain.

You are correct. But I can use it for the benefit of your soul. It is not your pain that has prompted you to come to Me every night. Nor is any physical limitation causing you to pray as much as you do, even if you don't think it is enough. There is progress. I am in control and I am not allowing you to take the controls back. You are aware of My doing a better job of ruling your life, but the carnal part of you keeps looking for another way. There

is no other way. No-one else knows you as I do. You do not even know yourself as well as I do. No one else can love you more than I do. And no-one else knows the plans I have for you. Have I not given you better for every part of your life that you had to give up?

The things I had to give up and the better part the Lord gave me for it:

My extended family in Hungary – a freer and more wonderful life in the United States

My dream of becoming a nun – a marvelous marriage and motherhood

My husband at his death – a closer relationship with God

My teaching career – the opportunity to care for my mother-in-law

My mother-in-law dying – the opportunity to fulfill a lifelong desire – becoming a nun

Being a nun – the opportunity to care for my own mother and knowing I was indeed doing God's will

The death of my mother – falling head-over-heels with a widower and finding out I was still able to experience such joy

That relationship I thought was a gift from God breaking up – realizing the Lord wants me to Himself

You are not disappointing me even when you are disappointed with yourself. I can handle it all. This is why I want you to work more on joyfulness. I provide many enjoyable moments in your life, but when you are discontented even with yourself, you miss the joy I have for you. Yes, you have many limitations. But when you focus on how much you can do despite them, instead of what you cannot do, you are much happier. Your patience has improved, and you are more disciplined than you give yourself credit for. And so, it should be.

When you take credit for such things, pride is ready to consume you. Being grateful for all the help you have, is so much better. There is still a hint of insecurity in your faith. You know that I love you, but have a hard time believing that you don't need to strive to earn that love. Trust Me that I can and will perfect you as I desire, and already see the perfection I will accomplish in you. No, you are not perfect yet. But if I am content with that, why shouldn't you be?

Once again, You are right, and I repent. I do trust You to keep working on me. You have been doing it for many years. And I do see the progress and thank You for it.

It works so much easier with your cooperation. But I have been known to do things in your life without your consent.

If it is worth anything, I now choose to cooperate with whatever You desire to do with me.

Thank you. Yes, you and I are both smiling. Hold on to the joy you are now receiving.

Thank You so much, Lord. You are awesome.

Lord, am I meddling in other people's lives too much, or is this what You want me to do?

Giving out helpful information is not meddling. Being concerned about others' needs is not meddling. If you insisted that they do something just because you think they should, that would be meddling. It is good that you are asking Me about these things. In the past, you would not have even thought of asking. You would have simply gone off and done things, and worried about whether others took your advice or not. Now, you can present ideas, and not be concerned about the outcomes.

Thank You, Lord. Help me to keep this attitude. As the next week progresses, please keep me connected to You. I know that when things get busy, I have a tendency to think I am in control, though I now realize that being in control is not helpful to me or to anyone I am dealing with. You need to be in control. Not me.

Saying that is easier than living it. There are some things you have control over. It is My will that you learn better self-control. The eating and becoming more active, though you are somewhat relying on Me to keep you focused, are things that are under your control. I appreciate your wanting My help, and I do provide it. But you have to choose to follow My leading and that is in your control. Other people's lives are not in your control. When you care about them, you are somewhat in the same position that I am with you in your efforts to gain self-control. I encourage, suggest, and help, but leave you to decide what you will do. Learn from Me.

Dear Jesus, thank You that I was not as unsettled yesterday, and more aware of Your love. Today I will try to attack the clutter in my house.

You see, there was no need to delve deeply into why you were reluctant to do certain things. Sometimes it is possible to overcome some difficulty without understanding it completely. Your inactivity was making you uncomfortable. You brought it to My attention, and then began to do the things you were avoiding. Now three of four hurdles have been overcome, and you have a plan in place to attack the fourth. C. S. Lewis's quote helped you. "If you are doing something you shouldn't, stop doing it. If you are not doing something you should, start doing it." It worked.

Yes, Lord, it did. And I am feeling much better about it all. Lord, I realize it was not just what I did or did not do that made the difference. You have been right here with me, even when I was not doing much. You also strengthened me to do what I did accomplish and gave me the help I needed when I realized I could not accomplish what I wanted to do. Thank You.

This is why you need to bring your problems to Me. Not every issue is because of your sins. You needed to see that there is help when you need it, and you don't need to demand it, but simply bring it to Me. My love is so much greater than you have ever known. But you are learning. It is good.

Thank You, Lord.

Sometimes waiting is a great part of self-control, as is submission and surrender to the Lord.

Dear Jesus, thank You for giving me a dream that the blindness in my right eye was healed. Though it was only a dream, the feeling was wonderful. I do believe You will someday heal it, but until You do, I will simply trust You and do what I can.

Lord, I remember when I was angry with You about people not being healed at our prayer meetings. We do believe You can heal, yet, so often You don't seem to do so. And we do not understand. Some get healed, and others don't. We do not see the healing You are doing inside them; we only see the outside. We don't want to speak negative things, we know You do not send sickness and pain and distress, but it is there, and we cannot seem to make it go away.

You are God, and we are not. We will wait for Your timing and purposes to manifest. We will trust in You whether we like what You are doing or not. And we will continue to ask, seek, and knock. We choose to cooperate with whatever You are doing and try not to second-guess Your purposes. Lord, I do submit and surrender, and continue my supplication for Your healing and power to be shown to an unbelieving world.

Maggie, I do understand the frustration. I was also frustrated with My disciples at times. And yes, I was frustrated that things did not happen as fast as I would have liked. Remember that I said I came to set a fire on the earth and how I wished it was already blazing? Some times and actions are set up in ways that only can be understood on the other side of eternity. Remember the man healed by Peter and John? Do you think he was not there as I passed by months or years before? Did I not see him or want to heal him? Yet he continued in his lameness until Peter and John came by.

Keep praying for healing and My intervention. Remember what you have heard. If you want to see hundreds healed, pray for thousands. My ways are not your ways, but you do have a part in My ways. Some healings take much longer than people wish for or like. Others are delayed because there is a greater good that is taking place inside. You pray.

Leave the results to Me. And do not think that I ignore your care and kindness toward those who still await My healing. I work wonders in the lives of those who care for the afflicted. You have seen the good results in the character of caregivers or relatives of the ill and disabled. I work with them, as well.

Lord, I see that I do not have to understand everything in order to obey and be a part of Your ways and plans. Help me to continue to trust You and remain in Your service. Use me however You see fit. I don't promise not to get frustrated or upset but help me to be and do whatever You desire.

That is a prayer I gladly answer.

Dear Jesus, thank You that You keep challenging yet encouraging me. I listened to a message yesterday, which did that. It said that prayer is hard. That it is the relationship that is important. That there are times of prayer when it is not at all pleasant or exhilarating. When you think you have been there for a very long time, but only a few minutes have actually passed. I have certainly experienced all this.

Lord, You have been so gracious to me, that I believe I do have a marvelous relationship with You. Please keep teaching me and drawing me closer. So often I am not sure if I am on the right track, but You are patient and kind, and find ways to either assure me or move me into place. Lord, I do thank You.

You have been pondering the natural vs. supernatural, the ordinary vs. the extraordinary. I do prefer to use natural and ordinary means most of the time. Much good character results in having to wait for natural and ordinary ways. Growth and healing usually take time.

Destruction is often quick. When you plant an acorn, it takes years for it to become a tree. But you can cut a tree down in less than a day. There is a time and place for miracles, but relationship is built through ordinary, natural ways. Accept the struggles. They provide great growth. You may not be able to see it immediately, but looking back, you will recognize that My ways work.

Trust, submission, and surrender, are only possible when you are assured that the One you trust, submit or surrender to, is truly wise and loving and cares for you completely. When you look to Me and know Me, your doubts will vanish. It is always My character that the tempter wants you to question. Once you believe that I am not all-loving and all good, then you can be convinced of almost anything. I know your desires, and when it is to your benefit, I fulfill them. But when I do not fulfill them as quickly as you desire, know that I have a bigger picture and plan that will be better.

Lord, You have proven to me that You are worthy of trust, submission, and surrender. But the three S's also include supplication, so I am glad You want us to keep asking for what we desire, and then let You decide how to answer. And I thank You that You do answer.

And I also give you peace when you trust Me. Peace is not inactivity. It is a deep confidence that I can handle whatever is happening. But I will not handle it alone; I will use you and others and make any necessary corrections. Faith, hope, love, trust, peace, and such virtues are developed through time and sometimes struggles. But they are well worth it all. This is why they are the fruits of the Spirit. They must grow and mature.

Lord, I seem to have nothing to talk about again tonight. Could You take over?

Try praying in the Spirit.

OK, come Holy Spirit _____

Lord, You just made me laugh again. It seems I do not know how to write in tongues.

It is just as well. It is not a written language. There are times I simply want to hear your voice.

And I look forward to the time when I can actually hear Yours. Though I am very grateful for being able to communicate with You this way.

There are limitations to the physical world. But they can be handled. There is a reason you cannot think of a topic to discuss. Martha needs to rest. Mary needs to take charge.

Is that why I have been so tired lately?

Yes, you need to give Me back the controls.

I did not even realize I had tried to take over.

I know. But you see that it is happening.

I do. Lord, help me submit and surrender again.

I can do that. The first step is to go back and rest in My arms. Then talk to Me in the morning.

I guess that is better than take two aspirin and call me in the morning.

Better, but similar. Hold on to Me. I still love you.

Thank You so much, Lord.

Lord, there is so much ugliness out in the world, but You have kept me safely tucked away in a garden of love. Thank You.

Yes, I have. I have come that you might have life and have it more abundantly. You do not have to be surrounded by the ugliness and evil that exists. You have seen and felt much pain throughout life, and I have brought you through it all. Now, I want you to focus on the beauty and goodness that is also in the world. I do not shield you from knowing about the muck and mire, but it is only that you can partner with Me and pray for those situations. I want you more aware of My love and care than the nastiness that also exists. The quiet life you now have is My gift to you.

And I do thank You for it. Forgive me for the times I have complained that it is too quiet.

I can handle your complaints. But I also appreciate the contentment you have learned over the years. Fr. Brady would be proud of you.

Lord, there You go again, making me smile. That is the word that nailed me to the wall on my first retreat. "Are you content?" At that time, I certainly was not, and I did not even know contentment was possible. But those three days of retreat at least gave me the desire for it.

Contentment should also be a fruit of the Spirit. It is a result of trust and self-control.

Lord, You are wonderful.

I gave up electronic games for Lent, and to fill up the time, I signed up for a couple of online courses with Institute of Catholic Culture. The first one was called Catholic Political Thought which was once a week for 17 weeks. Though I found it a bit challenging, I really liked it. Then there was a four- night course on St. Matthew's Gospel, and I was not very enthusiastic about that one.

How did you like the lecture on Matthew?

It was OK, but somehow, I was not as impressed as I thought I should be. But I will keep listening.

At least it is only for four days.

I listened to the second lecture on St. Matthew, and it was again OK, but not what I had hoped for. I guess I have come to expect it to be more personal and not academic encounters when I commit to such a teaching. But I suppose I am a bit unreasonable about this. I will continue to listen for the next two days and finish the course. I am glad I did not sign up for a much longer series of lectures.

I wonder why I am having such a negative reaction to this one, while I am enjoying the Thursday night class. It is also quite academic, but somehow it generates more awe and wonder within me. I suppose it does not matter whether I like these courses or not, what is important is that I learn whatever You want me to learn. And it is great to be learning again. For a long time, I seemed to have lost interest in learning at all. Thank You for rekindling that desire within me. Thank You also for the ability to learn.

Old age does not mean you have to live in the past. Yes, there are many memories, but life is more than just memories. Yes, your life has slowed down, but it is not over. Just because you are not as mobile as you used to be, does not mean you need to be bored and inactive. Giving up those computer games has awakened a part of you that you thought was dead.

It is all right to have preferences in what you are learning. Not every college course you took made you warm and fuzzy inside. Some of them you really enjoyed, while others you simply endured. You are now taking college level courses. And, yes, you can understand and follow them despite your disabilities. You had not expected that. You have been so focused on what you could no longer do, that you stopped even desiring to do anything at all. You are having your own personal awakening and revival. It is good.

I guess negativity sneaks in and we hardly even notice. I think it is Isaiah 43, one of my favorite chapters of Scripture You are showing me.

Yes, Is.43:18-19 *"Do not remember the former things or consider the things of old. I am about to do a new thing; now it springs forth; do you not perceive it?"* I am glad you do perceive it. Rejoice in this new perception.

Thank You, Lord. I suppose this is a part of self-control. Both trying new things, and persevering whether or not I like them.

Dear Jesus, thank You that the prayer meeting was very good. There were only four of us, but we did do a lot of intercession. Lord, there is so much trouble around. Last night on the news, many people were fearing civil war, not to mention world war with nuclear weapons. Lord, I am glad I got the teaching on which battles are ours, and which ones are Yours. This is Your battle. We, old ladies, are ready willing and somewhat able to assist You as channels of

Yours, to do whatever we can. Whether we live or die, we are Yours. I trust that You will bring order out of the chaos, but I also know that Your timeline is not the same as ours.

Communism lasted close to forty years in Hungary. If tyranny comes here, I doubt I can live forty more years to see its end. But whenever You move, I want to move with You. This country needs a resurrection. It sure looks like we are going through Holy Week not just recalling Your Passion and death, but also that of our nation, or even the world.

True, there is much turmoil. And you cannot be shielded from it. But neither are you to give in to all the fear that the enemy is trying to spread. There is no weakness in My army. Young or old, I provide all the strength you need for whatever assignment I give you. You are Mine. I will care for you and yours. I will not leave you or forsake you. Keep the balance of praise and joy with the supplication and vigilance. Your battle is not against flesh and blood, but against the spiritual forces of evil.

The joy of the Lord is your strength. You need to be filled daily with love and joy and peace. All that comes from Me. Even in war, the sun comes up each day, flowers still bloom. Find joy and love and peace in your life despite what is happening in the world. But do not neglect the intercessory prayer that is essential for My victory. And not only prayer, though much of that will be needed, but to continue to spread the love, joy, and peace I give you to others who do not yet know how to receive it.

I do not want a worried and fearful army. Watch and pray and listen for My commands. I have trained you well. You are stronger and more powerful than it would seem. Pray in the Spirit when you don't know what else you can do. If you listen to the news, pray through it. Then turn it off and pray some more. But every time you pray, remember that I am with you. In your prayers, you are agreeing with Me as to what should happen.

Let all the turmoil of the world draw you ever closer to Me and feel My love and appreciation for your company. Also draw closer to others who are also on My side. Encourage each other,

laugh with each other, heal each other's wounds. This is what soldiers do. But let no fear enter into your heart. I AM in charge.

You are indeed.

Easter Sunday"

It is now time to rejoice. The fruits of self-denial will now emerge. Whether or not you have noticed, you did draw much closer to Me through this Lent. Now, be ready to notice changes for the better. You received many blessings yesterday. It was a happy time. There are more yet to come. Continue in gratitude and prayer. You have seen that I do listen and answer. Sometimes not as quickly as you might like, but I do answer.

Remember that before My Passion and death, I could do many great and wonderful things. But after Resurrection, and before Pentecost, My actions were more amazing. And then, when My disciples received the Holy Spirit, the whole world was transformed. So, take the next 50 days to be full of awe and wonder. Then receive the Holy Spirit once again and transform the world.

This afternoon, I experienced a true joy, and wanted to tell family and friends, but could not reach any I tried. I realized that I could rejoice with You, but it still felt awkward. I am not yet at the point of being satisfied without other people to talk to. Lord, it feels terrible to say that, and I want to learn to rely on You more, but it is still true.

I have not asked you to be a hermit. It is natural for you to want to share joy with others. But you did try to come to Me with it, and it was a good beginning. Your need or desire to be with other people is not a flaw but a blessing. You have not been taken out of the world. Don't be ashamed of participating in the good things I provide. Sharing joy and gratitude with others is good.

What did the shepherd do when he found his lost sheep? He called his friends and they rejoiced together. The same with the woman who lost her coin and found it. She called her friends and they rejoiced together. This is a part of the Kingdom of God. I rejoice with you and with your friends when you are filled with joy. That you don't yet think to come to Me first, does not offend Me. You do come to Me, and I rejoice with you. Eventually, the timing will change. But for now, it is good.

Thank You so much, Lord. You are healing a part of my past as You tell me all this. My parents were offended that they were not the first to see my engagement ring, and I went through a great deal of pain about it then. I am so glad that You are not offended. Yet, I do want to put You first in everything. With Your help, I think it will happen.

It will, indeed. Now go and rest a bit more in My arms.

Dear Jesus, thank You that yesterday was a quiet restful day. Part of the night was difficult because of a horrendous headache, but thank You, that it is now much better. I did run out of things to do, so I turned on the TV, and during commercials, muted it and spent time in praise and thanksgiving. You seemed to bless that with You Presence, and I am grateful.

Yes, it is a good practice. You are finding Me more often during the day now. It is good and requires some self-control. I am working on filling the empty spaces in your life. Keep looking for Me. You will be surprised in how many ways you can find Me. I will give you projects to work on, but sometimes I just want your company. You wanted someone to watch TV with you last night and found that I can do that. We talked through the commercials. We can do that some more. Give Me your thoughts during those times, and I will continue to converse with you. Bring Me any problems you hear about. You will discover a new form of prayer.

Thank You, Lord. I will.

Lord, I want my will totally conformed to Yours. I suppose that is self-control. I do long for our extended conversations, but if right now that is not Your will, then I will be content with that. You are healing things inside me even without speaking. Thank You.

It is true. I am working on a different part of you than you are looking for. You want physical healing more than spiritual or emotional. I see the physical problems, but they will pass . I am more interested in the spiritual and emotional. Those last much longer. I want you to be immersed in My love and joy and peace. Not just for a few moments here or there, but continually. That does not consist of much talking. You need no great explanations, but experience. I am providing that. I want you to get used to it. Rejoice in it. Bask in it. Soak it in. Swim and folic in it. Wrap up in it. It is very good.

Thank You, Lord. I will stop complaining. Shorter times of conversation but longer times of experiencing Your love and joy and peace is finally making sense to me. Thank You.

Lord, somehow You are bringing order into my life. I thank You. I tried for so long to be more self-disciplined but seemed to always fail. But letting You be in control it seems so much simpler. And yet, I seem to so easily take back the controls and mess everything up. Please keep working on me.

I have no plans to stop. Everything you accomplished yesterday was because you resisted the initial resistance that came up within you. Build on that. Expect that your flesh will resist anything I suggest you should do. If you resist the resistance, peace and joy will come with each accomplishment. I am always with you to help and guide. Union is not just warm fuzzy feelings, but

also a relying on Me. As you continue to do this, I will begin to rely on you as well.

The communication between us will become natural, though unspoken. You have been worried that our conversations have become shorter, but I have been teaching you to dwell in My Presence even without conversation. There is progress whether you see it or not. Keep relying on Me. It is good.

Lord, I am feeling the love of learning once again. Things that seemed too hard to understand are now becoming clear. Thank You.

Dear Jesus, here I am, ready to have a conversation with You about modesty and chastity.

These are not easy subjects in the current culture.

How true! We have strayed so far from Your precepts, that a lot of people think these are at best outmoded, and at worst, impossibly ridiculous.

Let's start with modesty. What do you consider modesty?

Basically, I think of it as not calling attention to oneself. The dictionary gave me three definitions:

the quality or state of being <u>unassuming</u> or moderate in the estimation of one's abilities.

This would not be a false humility, but a realization that all we are and can accomplish begins with Your gifts to us. It would also involve giving credit to all others who assisted us in any achievements.

Notice that pride would be an opposite. There is pride that is sinful, and immediately seen as unattractive. But receiving credit for achievements need not be prideful, when modesty is present. Truth is the key.

1. the quality of being relatively moderate, limited, or small in amount, rate, or level.

Moderation and contentment are not as valued or understood in our society. As I have grown older, and met more limitations on my strength and stamina, I have grown to appreciate my modest way of life. I do not need or want many things others consider important. It allows me to be at peace, and seek only what You desire for me to have.

It also keeps you from several major vices. Jealousy, covetousness, gluttony, and even sloth. As long as you focus on what I want for you, and realize that I can meet all your needs, you can live with moderation and contentment.

behavior, manner, or appearance intended to avoid <u>impropriety</u> or indecency.

This seems to be the part that many in our world do not understand. Our children have not been taught the definitions of impropriety and indecency. When I was young, at age 19, a coworker gave me a great compliment which I have cherished in my memory ever since. He said, "Maggie, if it were fitting and proper, I could really love you." It was not fitting or proper, as he was already married, and he never did or said anything inappropriate to me, but I took it as a great compliment. In return, I did not say or do anything inappropriate, either.

Our world has become over-sexualized, and now overly confused. Lord, we need to relearn what is appropriate and decent. I do not think we need to become prudish or ignorant of reality, but there needs to be a balance.

Do not forget that God created them male and female for a purpose. That purpose is two-fold. The first is indeed attraction and pleasure, but the second is procreation, to be fruitful and multiply. Without the first, there would be no interest to achieve the second. When either is out of balance, chaos ensues. Sexual acts were created for marriage between a man and a woman. Without the lifelong commitment in marriage, it is disordered, or inappropriate. Many years ago, when you were teaching, you wrote about this. It is still something others need to hear.

A BRIEF HISTORY: The day after a particularly controversial television program, one of my students asked me (before class) if I had seen the show. As I have very strong opinions on the topic, my reply was that I did not, nor would I ever see such a show. This intrigued the student to ask why; and I, in my rather strong and tactless manner began to proclaim how all sex apart from a heterosexual marriage is sin, and must be avoided. This opened up an uproar from the student body that took several minutes to calm down and we decided that this was not really a good topic of discussion in a math class. We finally did get to the math, but I felt very uncomfortable with what had happened. I feel that in a Catholic school, I should be able to talk about moral issues, and try to steer the students toward sound moral decisions. I totally agree with and believe in the Catholic Church's wisdom in its teaching on sexuality and sexual conduct. However, the way I stated it was so negative that it did not glorify God at all. I made God sound like an unreasonable dictator, and not the loving and caring Person that I have come to know over the years. So as this was churning within me, I woke up very early the next morning and felt the Lord calling me to prayer. (I'm glad I responded.) What follows is the teaching I believe He inspired within me, and the next time I met with that class, I shared it with them. The class received it much better – at least they listened.

A WEDDING GIFT

When God created Adam and Eve, He did it out of love and care. He walked with them, talked with them, loved them, taught them, and had a good relationship with them. He gave them many, many good things. God provided for all their needs. He was good to them. The serpent, on the other hand, convinced Eve that God was not very good because He had made a tree in the garden from which they were not allowed to eat. Why did God put that tree there? Was He only testing their obedience? Was He unreasonable in this? We don't have all the answers, because His perfect plan was never revealed. It was cut short by the sin of our first parents, and we are still paying the price. We only have the serpent's interpretation of the reason for the existence of the tree of the Knowledge of Good and Evil. What if there was another reason for it to be there?

Could it be that the all-loving and all-good God of Adam and Eve was preparing that tree for something that had not yet happened? Could He have meant for them to gain more experience and knowledge of His provisions, love, and care before they had any knowledge of evil? Could He have wanted to strengthen and sustain them a bit longer before He discussed such a topic with them? Could it be that He wanted to tell them some things first, and then the fruit would truly make them wise? Could it be that the fruit was not yet ripe and would give them a sickness but later would be just fine? We do not know. What we do know is that they took something that was not theirs to take, something that they were expressly told not to eat, and they ate it. Did it make them wise? Well, they knew things they had not known before, but it did not help them at all. Did it kill them? Not immediately, but it broke their relationship with God, and they altered the original plan of their eternal life. They did eventually die. Was their life made any better by what they did? Definitely not. They lost the trust of God, and were thus banned from the garden and had to henceforth work hard.

Just like Adam and Eve, God has created us, cares for us, and gives us all the things we need for a good life. Life is not as easy for us as it was for Adam and Eve, but He loves us, and is good to us. As we grow up, He prepares a gift for us right before our eyes. At first, it means nothing to us, and we do not even notice it. Some of us begin to notice it earlier than others. Eventually, we find out and react to it in our own individual ways.

The gift is our sexuality. It is developing throughout our lives, and affects many aspects of our lives. The gift is in process, and though it looks very good at times, we need to wait until the Giver is ready for us to have it. God means to give the gift of sexual activity after the vows of marriage have been made (to each other before witnesses) by a man and a woman. It is a wedding gift. He has established marriage as a sacrament and He means to give us the gift at that time. He has been working on the gift as a piece of great artwork. He has also been teaching and preparing each partner in the marriage to be able to receive it and use it well. He even includes His own Presence in the gift to come and stay with the couple and help them through all the challenges that come with that state in life. He wants to be there to help, encourage, teach, inspire, and console each partner as they learn to live together, bring children into the world, and raise them.

The serpent is still around telling us the same old lies. "God is trying to keep something good away from you," he claims. We are no smarter than our first parents were. We steal what is not ours. It is meant to become something wonderful, but it is not ready yet, and we are not ready yet. Sex apart from a heterosexual marriage covenant, is as if the gift were being snatched out of the hands of God, and stolen before it is completely finished. The stolen gift also does not have the Giver attached. The Giver is rejected in the process of the theft. He is considered unkind, unfair, as one taunting with a forbidden fruit and ready to pounce on and punish if we should take the bait. Then when problems come, we blame Him.

When this gift is stolen and used in ways it was not meant to be, all sorts of problems arise. Some are so great that they are life-threatening. Others do not surface for many years. Yet, there is always a way to return to God, acknowledge our mistake, and submit to His plans. Sometimes we wait so long that His original plan cannot take place. He forms another plan that will still be for our good, and if we cooperate with His grace, our lives will be full and good.

Some people are invited to choose a different gift. In their choice, they willingly give up the right to the wedding present. God also gives them a great and wonderful gift that has all the grace and Giver attached to help them live the commitments they make. Still others are not drawn to the gift or do not find a partner with whom to share it. They are given all they need as well. Some people find themselves greatly tempted to take and use the gift in a way it is not meant to be used. They need to continually turn to God to get the grace to overcome the temptation. He is good and gracious enough to give the necessary strength and grace to avoid the things that will eventually hurt us and others.

In our society, we have not been convinced that God even exists, much less that He is all good and loving and kind. Our generation has portrayed Him more as the Great Policeman in the sky who is ready to hit you on the head if you make a mistake. We see Him as the "never satisfied" slave-driver. Many of us have believed the lie that God does not want our good, but is unreasonable. Perhaps if we give Him a little more credit for the good things in life, and look for His purposes instead of assigning bad intentions to Him, we could see things differently. This is why we are not to condemn others. If we tell people that God loves them, He will let them know in a much gentler and more loving way if they are wrong. He is a master at bringing good out of the most horrible of circumstances and is ever waiting and ready to give us more good than we ever imagined.

My final fruit to discuss is chastity. The dictionary definition I read on the computer is:

> "Chastity is a virtue that means abstaining from sexual activity that is considered immoral or from any sexual activity, depending on one's life situation. It can also mean purity in conduct and intention, or restraint and simplicity in design or expression."

Many people in our culture do not even know that chastity is possible. It is. Our world has become so sex-oriented, that it needs to be re-taught. Sexuality is a beautiful and wonderful gift from God under the proper circumstances.

Consider that sexual activity is like driving a car. But there has to be proper conditions met in order to become what it was meant to be. In order to drive a car, there must be a car to be driven. If there is no car, driving it is not possible. One can live a perfectly full and good life without ever driving a car. It is not a right, but a privilege. But without a car, other activities take the place of driving. Some who do not drive, live in places where it is not necessary. Others are too young, or disabled to drive. Yet they manage to live full and productive lives. This is like the single life.

Or as in my life, widowhood, and legal blindness.

Others have to wait for the proper time and training and license even if there is a car available. When all three are accomplished, driving is permitted and proper. This is like marriage.

You need to be mature enough to make a life-time commitment, be informed about the responsibilities involved, and actually make that commitment.

So, chastity is following the rules both for the good of oneself and the good of others. I would not want to be around someone who is driving without a license. But what about those who take a vow of chastity?

They choose a different license. It is a different state in life. They choose to refrain from sexual activity in order to focus on service to God and others. It may take much self-control at times, but faithfulness to the vow and the gift of grace makes it possible.

Lord, both modesty and chastity seem to have a lot to do with self-control.

Yes, and self-control is uniquely given to humanity. It is a gift, though it is often seen as a restriction or a curse. It is a part of true liberty. Humans do not need to be enslaved by drives, urges, or even desires. They have the freedom and capability to choose to set them aside for a greater good. But as self-control is a fruit of the Spirit, it needs to grow and be nurtured. It has to be taught to the young, and continually practiced in maturity.

Self-control is the fruit of the Spirit that is either motivated by or enhances the other fruits. When motivated by love, it becomes almost natural and simple. When one loves another, there are certain words or actions that are modified or avoided in order to defer to the beloved. The joy and peace in the relationship far outweigh the effort to control oneself. Patience is also akin to self-control. Waiting for the proper time for a desired thing is often difficult. Kindness, goodness, generosity, and faithfulness are also great motivations for self-control. Thus, the entire fruit salad comes together. Each fruit is good in itself, but when put together, it becomes a masterpiece.

Epilogue

Who am I and why I am writing spiritual books?

I consider myself an average, middle-class Christian, American. But each of these adjectives have had changes, fluctuations, evolutions, and episodes. I will tell you only the highlights here, but if I live long enough to publish a third book, it will be a more comprehensive autobiography.

From 1947 to 1956, I was a Hungarian child living in Budapest. In 1956, there was a revolution in Hungary, and the borders were not as securely guarded by the Soviet Communist government, and many people, including my immediate family escaped to Austria. There, we were given shelter and food and stayed in refugee camps for several weeks. Through the grace and somewhat miraculous acts of God, we were able to legally emigrate to Washington D.C.

At every turn, we were wonderfully treated. America was full of very kind and generous people. My sister and I were enrolled in a Catholic grade school and became Americanized. We loved the more easy-going lifestyle versus the very formal European way of life.

At age 11, I realized God had led us to this marvelous country and felt I wanted to give my life to Him in return. Since we were taught by nuns, I thought I would like to become one when I grew up. This was my one ambition in life until I met my husband at age 19.

I studied hard, made sure I learned the language so no-one could tell I was not American born. I also enjoyed learning more and more about my Catholic faith, as in Hungary my parents had to sneak a priest into our home to prepare us for basic Sacraments. I also became quite good at math. Before I could speak English, if they put a math problem on the board, I could do that without having to speak. There is nothing like success to make one like something.

After high school, I worked for a year, met my husband, went to college for a year, got married, lost my faith, finished college, and became a math teacher. When our first son was born, I started looking for the faith I had lost. God found me through the Charismatic Renewal in 1975. He restored my faith, but this time it came back with roots.

I remained Catholic but was delighted to learn all I could about Scripture and a relationship with God from many Protestant, Pentecostal, and Messianic Jewish sources. I was taught to "eat the meat and spit out the bones." In other words, use what you can, and set aside the rest.

We had two more sons, and in 1995, my husband died of a heart attack. By then, I was teaching at the Catholic high school where my youngest son was a freshman. By this time, I was under spiritual direction, and had grown a lot in my faith. I was teaching Algebra and Jewish Scriptures.

I became the caretaker for my mother-in-law who developed Alzheimer's and I took night classes and earned a master's degree in education while still teaching. A year later, I became ill, and needed to give up my teaching job. After the death of my mother-in-law, and my partial recovery, the desire for full-time ministry returned, and I entered a convent and became Sister Magdalena. I worked for two years with the Little Sisters of Jesus and Mary, but then was told to go home and be a grandmother, as my oldest son had just had a daughter, and they were expecting another child. My health was also deteriorating, and the sisters did not think they could care for me as things might get worse.

When I returned home, I found my own mother, by now widowed, also needed much care. Soon I had her living with me, and I cared for her until her death in 2011.

I started journaling my prayer life in 1989. From the time I returned to faith in 1975 until then, I struggled with keeping a consistent prayer life. I found that writing what I wanted to say to God, and then writing what I thought He might say to me, would help me. It did. It slowed my thinking down and kept my concentration well enough that marvelous ideas showed up on my notebooks. I felt I found a two-way communication with God. Every time I re-read what I had written, I was amazed and in awe of how gentle, kind, and encouraging He was to me. I continued to study and read and listen to teachings that helped me to grow in my relationship with Him. I wanted total union. I still do.

Some of my writings seemed too good to keep to myself. But I did not know how to effectively share them. I found a lovely lady to help me edit the 1502 pages I had accumulated by 2016 but knew that was not feasible to publish. During the Covid crisis in 2020, I finally had the inspiration to cut and paste entries that pertained to my own goals in life that became my life prayer. Thus, Grace and Gratitude, Developing Personal Prayer was published in 2022. By this time, I was legally blind and had stopped writing by hand, as I could not read my own work.

But my sister encouraged me to start writing again, and the Lord was kind enough to give me more teachings, so Spiritual Fruit Salad, Relationship with God emerged.

My hope is that in seeing how God has taught and worked in my life, you can also develop your own unique and close personal relationship with the entire Trinity, Father, Jesus, and Holy Spirit. If you already have such a relationship, I hope my writings will edify, amuse, or encourage you. Above all, I want to glorify and magnify Him. He has been very good to me.

www.ingramcontent.com/pod-product-compliance
Lightning Source LLC
Chambersburg PA
CBHW051141120626
46547CB00012B/900